THE GREAT BRITISH COOKBOOK

Hilaire Walden

THE GREAT BRITISH COOKBOOK

✠══ **Hilaire Walden** ══✠

Over 130 traditional family recipes – step by step

Photography by Steve Baxter

🐧 **Dolphin Publications** 🐧

This edition specially produced for
Dolphin Publications
Bridge Mills Business Park
Langley Road South
Pendleton
Salford M6 6EL

First published by Dolphin Publications in 1994
and exclusive to them in the UK.

ISBN 1-873762-12-7

Editorial Director: Joanna Lorenz
Series Editor: Linda Fraser
Designers: Tony Paine and Roy Prescott
Photographer: Steve Baxter
Food For Photography: Wendy Lee
Props Stylist: Kirsty Rawlings

Printed and bound in Singapore

Acknowledgements
For their assistance in the publication of this book
the publishers wish to thank:

Kenwood Appliances Plc
New Lane
Havant
Hants P09 2NH

Prestige
Prestige House
22–26 High Street
Egham, Surrey
TW20 9DU

Magimix
115A High Street
Godalming, Surrey
GU7 1AQ

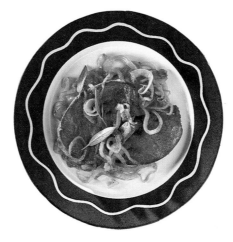

CONTENTS

SOUPS

Britain's rich tradition of soup-making encompasses a wide range of different recipes, from light Country Vegetable Soup to warming Split Pea and Bacon Soup, from fragrant puréed Green Pea and Mint Soup to savoury Smoked Haddock and Potato Soup and spicy Mulligatawny. There are also hearty meat-and-vegetable dishes that are akin to stews, such as Cock-a-leekie and Scotch Broth. Many of the soups evolved in the past as staple foods of the poor, often eaten with bread as the main part of a meal. Today, too, a soup can form the core of a light, convenient lunch or supper. Alternatively, serve soups as the first course of a meal, following the practice established in Victorian times.

GREEN PEA AND MINT SOUP

This soup is equally delicious cold. Instead of reheating it after puréeing, leave it to cool and then chill lightly in the fridge. Stir in the swirl of cream just before serving.

INGREDIENTS

Serves 4
50g/2oz/4 tbsp butter
4 spring onions (scallions), chopped
450g/1 lb fresh or frozen peas
600ml/1 pint/2½ cups chicken or
 vegetable stock
2 large mint sprigs
600 ml/1 pint/2½ cups milk
pinch of sugar (optional)
salt and pepper
single cream, to serve
small mint sprigs, to garnish

1 Heat the butter in a large saucepan, add the spring onions (scallions), and cook gently until softened but not coloured.

FREEZER NOTE
The soup can be frozen for up to two months after step 2. Allow it to thaw in the fridge before puréeing and reheating.

2 Stir the peas into the pan, add the stock and mint and bring to the boil. Cover and simmer very gently for about 30 minutes for fresh peas or 15 minutes if you are using frozen peas, until the peas are very tender. Remove about 45ml/3 tbsp of the peas using a slotted spoon, and reserve for the garnish.

3 Pour the soup into a food processor or blender, add the milk and purée until smooth. Then return the soup to the pan and reheat gently. Season to taste, adding a pinch of sugar, if liked.

4 Pour the soup into bowls. Swirl a little cream into each, then garnish with mint and the reserved peas.

LEEK AND POTATO SOUP

The chopped vegetables in this recipe produce a chunky soup. If you prefer a smooth texture, press the mixture through a sieve (strainer) or purée it in a food mill.

INGREDIENTS

Serves 4
50g/2oz/4 tbsp butter
2 leeks, chopped
1 small onion, finely chopped
350g/12oz potatoes, chopped
900ml/1½ pints/3¾ cups chicken or
  vegetable stock
salt and pepper

1 Heat 25g/1oz/2 tbsp of the butter in a large saucepan, add the leeks and onions and cook gently, stirring occasionally, for about 7 minutes, until softened but not browned.

COOK'S TIP
Don't use a food processor to purée this soup as it can give the potatoes a gluey consistency.

2 Add the potatoes to the pan and cook, stirring occasionally, for 2–3 minutes, then add the stock and bring to the boil. Cover the pan and simmer gently for 30–35 minutes, until the vegetables are very tender.

3 Adjust the seasoning, remove the pan from the heat and stir in the remaining butter in small pieces. Serve hot with crusty bread.

COCK-A-LEEKIE

This ancient soup recipe – it is known from as long ago as 1598 – originally included beef as well as chicken. In the past it would have been made from an old cock bird, hence the name.

INGREDIENTS

Serves 4–6
2 chicken portions, about 275g/10oz
*   each*
1.2 litres/2 pints/5 cups chicken stock
bouquet garni
4 leeks
8–12 prunes, soaked
salt and pepper
soft buttered rolls, to serve

1 Gently cook the chicken, stock and bouquet garni for 40 minutes.

2 Cut the white part of the leeks into 2.5cm/1in slices and thinly slice a little of the green part.

3 Add the white part of the leeks and the prunes to the saucepan and cook gently for 20 minutes, then add the green part of the leeks and cook for a further 10–15 minutes.

4 Discard the bouquet garni. Remove the chicken from the pan, discard the skin and bones and chop the flesh. Return the chicken to the pan and season the soup. Heat the soup through, then serve hot with soft buttered rolls.

SCOTCH BROTH

Sustaining and warming, Scotch Broth is custom-made for chilly Scottish weather, and makes a delicious winter soup anywhere.

INGREDIENTS

Serves 6–8
1kg/2 lb lean neck of lamb, cut into
*   large, even-sized chunks*
1.75 litres/3 pints/7½ cups water
1 large onion, chopped
50g/2oz/¼ cup pearl barley
bouquet garni
1 large carrot, chopped
1 turnip, chopped
3 leeks, chopped
½ small white cabbage, shredded
salt and pepper

1 Put the lamb and water into a large saucepan and bring to the boil. Skim off the scum, then stir in the onion, barley and bouquet garni.

2 Bring the soup back to the boil, then partly cover the saucepan and simmer gently for 1 hour. Add the remaining vegetables and the seasoning to the pan. Bring to the boil, partly cover again and simmer for about 35 minutes until the vegetables are tender.

3 Remove surplus fat from the top of the soup, then serve hot, sprinkled with chopped parsley.

COUNTRY VEGETABLE SOUP

To ring the changes, vary the vegetables according to what is in season.

INGREDIENTS

Serves 4
50g/2oz/4 tbsp butter
1 onion, chopped
2 leeks, sliced
2 celery sticks, sliced
2 carrots, sliced
2 small turnips, chopped
4 ripe tomatoes, skinned and chopped
1 litre/1¼ pints/4 cups chicken, veal or
   vegetable stock
bouquet garni
115g/4oz green beans, chopped
salt and pepper
chopped herbs such as tarragon,
   thyme, chives and parsley, to garnish

1 Heat the butter in a large saucepan, add the onion and leeks and cook gently until soft but not coloured.

2 Add the celery, carrots and turnips and cook for 3–4 minutes, stirring occasionally. Stir in the tomatoes and stock, add the bouquet garni and simmer for about 20 minutes.

3 Add the beans to the soup and cook until all the vegetables are tender. Season to taste and serve garnished with chopped herbs.

SPLIT PEA AND BACON SOUP

Another name for this soup is 'London Particular', from the dense fogs for which the city used to be notorious. The fogs in turn were named 'pea-soupers'.

INGREDIENTS

Serves 4
15g/½oz/1 tbsp butter
115g/4oz smoked back bacon,
   chopped
1 large onion, chopped
1 carrot, chopped
1 celery stick, chopped
75g/3oz/scant ½ cup split peas
1.2 litres/2 pints/5 cups chicken stock
salt and pepper
2 thick slices firm bread, buttered and
   without crusts
2 slices streaky bacon

1 Heat the butter in a saucepan, add the back bacon and cook until the fat runs. Stir in the onion, carrot and celery and cook for 2–3 minutes.

2 Add the split peas followed by the stock. Bring to the boil, stirring occasionally, then cover and simmer for 45–60 minutes.

3 Meanwhile, preheat the oven to 180°C/350°F/Gas 4 and bake the bread for about 20 minutes, until crisp and brown, then cut into cubes.

4 Grill the streaky bacon until very crisp, then chop finely.

5 When the soup is ready, season to taste and serve hot with chopped bacon and croutons scattered on each portion.

SMOKED HADDOCK AND POTATO SOUP

The traditional name for this soup is 'cullen skink'. A cullen is the 'seatown' or port district of a town, while 'skink' means stock or broth.

INGREDIENTS

Serves 6
1 Finnan haddock, about 350g/12oz
1 onion, chopped
bouquet garni
900ml/1½ pints/3¾ cups water
500g/1¼ lb potatoes, quartered
600ml/1 pint/2½ cups milk
40g/1½oz/3 tbsp butter
salt and pepper
snipped chives, to garnish

1 Put the haddock, onion, bouquet garni and water into a large saucepan and bring to the boil. Skim the scum from the surface, then cover the pan. Reduce the heat and poach for 10–15 minutes, until the haddock flakes easily.

2 Lift the haddock from the pan, using a fish slice, and remove the skin and bones. Flake the flesh and reserve. Return the skin and bones to the pan and simmer, uncovered, for 30 minutes.

3 Strain the fish stock and return to the pan, then add the potatoes and simmer for about 25 minutes, or until tender. Remove the potatoes from the pan using a slotted spoon. Add the milk to the pan and bring to the boil.

4 Meanwhile, mash the potatoes with the butter, then whisk into the milk in the pan until thick and creamy. Add the flaked fish to the pan and adjust the seasoning. Sprinkle with chives and serve at once with crusty bread.

MULLIGATAWNY SOUP

Mulligatawny (which means 'pepper water') was introduced into England in the late eighteenth century by members of the army and colonial service returning home from India.

INGREDIENTS

Serves 4

50g/2oz/4 tbsp butter or 60ml/4 tbsp oil
2 large chicken joints, about 350g/ 12oz each
1 onion, chopped
1 carrot, chopped
1 small turnip, chopped
about 15ml/1 tbsp curry powder, to taste
4 cloves
6 black peppercorns, lightly crushed
50g/2oz/¼ cup lentils
900ml/1½ pints/3¾ cups chicken stock
40g/1½oz/¼ cup sultanas (golden raisins)
salt and pepper

1 Melt the butter or heat the oil in a large saucepan, then brown the chicken over a brisk heat. Transfer the chicken to a plate.

COOK'S TIP
Choose red split lentils for the best colour, although either green or brown lentils could also be used.

2 Add the onion, carrot and turnip to the pan and cook, stirring occasionally, until lightly coloured. Stir in the curry powder, cloves and peppercorns and cook for 1–2 minutes, then add the lentils.

3 Pour the stock into the pan, bring to the boil, then add the sultanas (golden raisins) and chicken and any juices from the plate. Cover and simmer gently for about 1¼ hours.

4 Remove the chicken from the pan and discard the skin and bones. Chop the flesh, return to the soup and reheat. Check the seasoning before serving the soup piping hot.

STARTERS AND SNACKS

Recipes suitable for present-day first courses and snacks are culled from a variety of traditional sources. Potting and smoking fish were methods of preserving developed in the days before refrigeration, providing us with Potted Shrimps and several delicious smoked fish recipes. There are regional specialities such as Welsh Rabbit, and dishes like Stuffed Mushrooms that make use of seasonal foods. A number of the dishes used to be breakfast fare – among them Devilled Kidneys – while others, such as Savoury Scrambled Eggs and Mussels In Bacon, used to be served as 'savouries' to round off a formal dinner.

SMOKED TROUT SALAD

Horseradish is as good a partner to smoked trout as it is to roast beef. In this recipe it combines with yogurt to make a delicious light salad dressing.

INGREDIENTS

Serves 4
1 oakleaf or other red lettuce
225g/8oz small tomatoes, cut into thin
*   wedges*
½ cucumber, peeled and thinly sliced
4 smoked trout fillets, about
*   200g/7oz each, skinned and flaked*

For The Dressing
pinch of English mustard powder
15–20ml/3–4 tsp white wine vinegar
30ml/2 tbsp light olive oil
100ml/3½ fl oz/scant ½ cup plain
*   (natural) yogurt*
about 30ml/2 tbsp grated fresh or
*   bottled horseradish*
pinch of caster (superfine) sugar

1 First, make the dressing. Mix together the mustard powder and vinegar, then gradually whisk in the oil, yogurt, horseradish and sugar. Set aside for 30 minutes.

COOK'S TIP
Salt should not be necessary in this recipe because of the saltiness of the smoked trout.

2 Place the lettuce leaves in a large bowl. Stir the dressing again, then pour half of it over the leaves and toss lightly using two spoons.

3 Arrange the lettuce on four individual plates with the tomatoes, cucumber and trout. Spoon over the remaining dressing and serve at once.

STUFFED MUSHROOMS

Serves 4

275g/10oz spinach, stalks removed
400g/14oz medium cap mushrooms
25g/1oz/2 tbsp butter, plus extra for
  brushing
25g/1oz bacon, chopped
½ small onion, finely chopped
75ml/5 tbsp double (heavy) cream
about 60ml/4 tbsp finely grated
  Cheddar cheese
2 tbsp fresh breadcrumbs
salt and pepper
sprig of parsley, to garnish

1 Preheat the oven to 190°C/375°F/
Gas 5. Butter a baking dish. Wash
but do not dry the spinach. Place it in
a pan and cook, stirring occasionally,
until wilted and no liquid is visible.

2 Tip the spinach into a colander and
squeeze out as much liquid as
possible. Chop finely. Snap the stalks
from the mushrooms and chop the
stalks finely.

3 Melt the butter, then cook the
bacon, onion and mushroom stalks
for about 5 minutes. Stir in the
spinach, cook for a moment or two,
then remove the pan from the heat and
stir in the cream and seasoning.

4 Brush the mushroom caps with
melted butter, then place, gills
uppermost, in a single layer in the
baking dish.

5 Divide the spinach mixture among
the mushrooms. Mix together the
cheese and breadcrumbs, sprinkle over
the mushrooms, then bake for about
20 minutes, until the mushrooms are
tender. Serve warm, garnished with a
sprig of parsley.

WATCHPOINT
It is important to make sure that
all the surplus liquid is squeezed
out of the spinach, otherwise the
stuffing will be too soggy.

PEARS AND STILTON

Stilton is the classic British blue cheese, but you could use blue Cheshire instead, or even a non-British cheese such as Gorgonzola.

INGREDIENTS

Serves 4
4 ripe pears, lightly chilled
75g/3oz blue Stilton cheese
50g/2oz curd (medium fat soft cheese)
pepper
watercress sprigs, to garnish

For The Dressing
45ml/3 tbsp light olive oil
15ml/1 tbsp lemon juice
10ml/½ tbsp toasted poppy seeds
salt and pepper

1 First make the dressing, place the olive oil, lemon juice, poppy seeds and seasoning in a screw-topped jar and shake together until emulsified.

2 Cut the pears in half lengthways, then scoop out the cores and cut away the calyx from the rounded end.

3 Beat together the Stilton, soft cheese and a little pepper. Divide this mixture among the cavities in the pears.

4 Shake the dressing to mix it again, then spoon it over the pears. Serve garnished with watercress.

POTTED SHRIMPS

The tiny brown shrimps traditionally used for potting are very fiddly to peel. Since they are rare nowadays, it is easier to use peeled cooked prawns (shrimps) instead.

INGREDIENTS

Serves 4
225g/8oz shelled shrimps
225g/8oz/1 cup butter
pinch of ground mace
salt
cayenne pepper
dill (dillweed) sprigs, to garnish
lemon wedges and thin slices of brown
  bread and butter, to serve

1 Chop a quarter of the shrimps. Melt 115g/4oz/½ cup of the butter slowly, carefully skimming off any foam that rises to the surface.

2 Stir all the shrimps, the mace, salt and cayenne into the pan and heat gently without boiling. Pour the shrimps and butter mixture into four individual pots and leave to cool.

3 Heat the remaining butter in a clean small saucepan, then carefully spoon the clear butter over the shrimps, leaving behind the sediment.

4 Leave until the butter is almost set, then place a dill (dillweed) sprig in the centre of each pot. Leave to set completely, then cover and chill.

5 Transfer the shrimps to room temperature 30 minutes before serving with lemon wedges and thin slices of brown bread and butter.

LEEKS WITH MUSTARD DRESSING

Pencil-slim baby leeks are increasingly available nowadays, and are beautifully tender. Use three or four of these smaller leeks per serving.

INGREDIENTS

Serves 4

8 slim leeks, each about 13cm/5in long
5–10ml/1–2 tsp Dijon mustard
10ml/2 tsp white wine vinegar
1 hard-boiled egg, halved lengthways
75ml/5 tbsp light olive oil
10ml/2 tsp chopped fresh parsley
salt and pepper

1 Steam the leeks over a pan of boiling water until just tender.

2 Meanwhile, stir together the mustard and vinegar in a bowl. Scoop the egg yolk into the bowl and mash thoroughly into the vinegar mixture using a fork.

3 Gradually work in the oil to make a smooth sauce, then season to taste.

4 Lift the leeks out of the steamer and place on several layers of kitchen paper, then cover the leeks with several more layers of kitchen paper and pat dry.

5 Transfer the leeks to a serving dish while still warm, spoon the dressing over them and leave to cool. Finely chop the egg white using a large sharp knife, then mix with the chopped fresh parsley and scatter over the leeks. Chill until ready to serve.

COOK'S TIP
Although this dish is served cold, make sure that the leeks are still warm when you pour over the dressing so that they will absorb the mustardy flavours.

SMOKED HADDOCK PATE

Arbroath smokies are small haddock that are beheaded and gutted but not split before being salted and hot-smoked.

INGREDIENTS

Serves 6
3 large Arbroath smokies, about 225g/
  8oz each
275g/10oz/1¼ cups medium fat soft
  cheese
3 eggs, beaten
30–45ml/2–3 tbsp lemon juice
pepper
sprigs of chervil, to garnish
lemon wedges and lettuce leaves,
  to serve

1 Preheat the oven to 160°C/325°F/ Gas 3. Butter six ramekin dishes.

2 Lay the smokies in a baking dish and heat through in the oven for 10 minutes. Carefully remove the skin and bones from the smokies, then flake the flesh into a bowl.

COOK'S TIP
There should be no need to add salt to this recipe, as smoked haddock is naturally salty – taste the mixture to check.

3 Mash the fish with a fork and work in the cheese, then the eggs. Add lemon juice and pepper to taste.

4 Divide the fish mixture among the ramekins and place in a roasting tin. Pour hot water into the roasting tin to come halfway up the dishes. Bake for 30 minutes, until just set.

5 Allow to cool for 2–3 minutes, then run a knife point around the edge of each dish and invert on to a warmed plate. Garnish with chervil sprigs and serve with the lemon and lettuce.

EGGY BREAD WITH CHEESE

Although very simple – or perhaps because of its simplicity – Eggy Bread has been popular for generations, and is enjoyed by all age groups.

INGREDIENTS

Serves 2–4

3 eggs
75ml/5 tbsp milk
45ml/3 tbsp chopped fresh herbs such as tarragon, parsley and chervil
4 slices bread
4 slices Red Leicester cheese
40g/1½oz/3 tbsp butter
salt and pepper

1 Lightly beat the eggs, milk, herbs and seasoning together. Pour into a large shallow dish.

2 Cut the crusts from the bread and make into sandwiches with the cheese. Cut them in half to make triangles, then dip both sides of each sandwich in the milk mixture.

3 Heat the butter in a frying pan, add the bread and fry until golden on both sides. Serve at once.

SAVOURY SCRAMBLED EGGS

Known as 'Scotch Woodcock', these eggs were popular in Victorian and Edwardian times as a savoury served instead of cheese at the end of a meal.

INGREDIENTS

Serves 2

2 slices bread
40g/1½oz/3 tbsp butter, plus extra for spreading
anchovy paste such as Gentleman's Relish
2 eggs, beaten
2 egg yolks
60–90ml/4–6 tbsp cream or milk
salt and pepper
anchovy fillets cut into strips, and paprika for garnish

1 Toast the bread, spread with butter and anchovy paste, then remove the crusts and cut into fingers. Keep warm, while you make the scrambled eggs.

2 Melt the rest of the butter in a non-stick saucepan, then stir in the eggs, egg yolks, cream or milk, a little salt, and pepper. Heat very gently, stirring constantly, until the mixture begins to thicken.

3 Remove the pan from the heat and continue to stir until the mixture becomes creamy.

4 Spoon the egg mixture evenly on to the toast fingers and garnish with strips of anchovy fillet and a sprinkling of paprika. Serve immediately.

WELSH RABBIT

This delicious supper dish is made from toast and a flavourful cheese sauce. It doesn't, as the name might suggest, contain any meat. It is sometimes called 'Welsh rarebit', although 'rabbit' seems to have been the original name. To turn Welsh Rabbit into Buck Rabbit, top each portion with a poached egg.

INGREDIENTS

Serves 4
4 thick slices of bread, crusts removed
25g/1oz/2 tbsp butter
225g/8oz/2 cups grated mature
  Cheddar cheese
5ml/1 tsp English mustard powder
few drops Worcestershire sauce
60ml/4 tbsp brown ale, beer or milk

1 Preheat the grill (broiler). Toast the bread until golden, then place in a single layer in a wide, shallow baking dish. Keep warm.

2 Melt the butter in a small to medium, heavy-based, preferably non-stick saucepan over a very low heat, or in a bowl placed over a saucepan of hot water.

COOK'S TIP
Use a strong flavoured cheese so the topping has plenty of flavour.

3 Stir the grated Cheddar cheese, English mustard powder and Worcestershire sauce into the melted butter, then slowly pour in the ale, beer or milk in a steady stream, stirring the cheese mixture all the time until very well blended.

4 Spoon the cheese mixture onto the toast then place under the hot grill (broiler) until bubbling and golden. Serve immediately.

DEVILLED KIDNEYS

'Devilled' dishes are always hot and spicy. If you have time, mix the spicy ingredients together in advance to give the flavours time to mingle and mature.

INGREDIENTS

Serves 4
10ml/2 tsp Worcestershire sauce
15ml/1 tbsp prepared English mustard
15ml/1 tbsp lemon juice
15ml/1 tbsp tomato purée (paste)
pinch of cayenne pepper
40g/1½ oz/3 tbsp butter
1 shallot, finely chopped
8 lambs' kidneys, skinned, halved and cored
salt and pepper
15ml/1 tbsp chopped fresh parsley, to garnish

1 Mix the Worcestershire sauce, mustard, lemon juice, tomato purée (paste), cayenne pepper and salt together to make a sauce.

2 Melt the butter in a frying pan, add the shallot and cook, stirring occasionally, until softened but not coloured.

COOK'S TIP
To remove the cores from the kidneys, use kitchen scissors, rather than a knife – you will find that it is much easier.

3 Stir the kidney halves into the shallot in the pan and cook over a medium–high heat for about 3 minutes on each side.

4 Pour the sauce over the kidneys and quickly stir so they are evenly coated. Serve immediately, sprinkled with chopped parsley.

CRAB SAVOURY

INGREDIENTS

Serves 4

25g/1oz/2 tbsp butter
1 small onion, finely chopped
50g/2oz/1 firmly packed cup fresh
  brown breadcrumbs
225g/8oz crabmeat
150ml/¼pt/⅔ cup soured
  (sour) cream
10–15ml/2–3tsp prepared mustard
pinch of cayenne pepper
squeeze of lemon juice
75ml/5 tbsp finely grated
  Cheddar cheese
salt

1 Melt the butter in a saucepan, then cook the onion gently until soft but not brown. Meanwhile, preheat the grill (broiler).

2 Stir the breadcrumbs, crabmeat, soured (sour) cream and mustard into the onions. Add a generous sprinkling of cayenne pepper, lemon juice and salt to taste. Heat through gently, stirring carefully.

3 Spoon the crab mixture into a baking dish, sprinkle the cheese over the top and place under the hot grill (broiler) until golden and bubbling.

SMOKED MACKEREL PATE

The pâté can be flavoured with horseradish, if liked.

INGREDIENTS

Serves 4

275g/10oz smoked mackerel fillet,
  skinned
90ml/6 tbsp soured (sour) cream
75g/3oz/6 tbsp unsalted (sweet) butter,
  softened
30ml/2 tbsp chopped fresh parsley
15–30 ml/1–2 tbsp lemon juice
pepper
chicory leaves and parsley, to garnish
fingers of toast, to serve

COOK'S TIP
For a less rich (and lower calorie) version of this pâté, substitute 200g/7oz/scant 1 cup low fat soft cheese or sieved cottage cheese for the soured (sour) cream.

1 Remove any bones from the mackerel, then mash it using a fork.

2 Work the soured (sour) cream and butter into the mackerel until smooth. Stir in the parsley, and add lemon juice and pepper to taste.

3 Pack the mackerel mixture into a dish or bowl, then cover tightly and chill overnight.

4 About 30 minutes before serving, remove the pâté from the fridge to allow it to return to room temperature. To serve, spoon on to individual plates and garnish with chicory leaves and parsley. Serve with fingers of toast.

MUSSELS IN BACON

This recipe is based on the well-known 'angels on horseback' in which oysters are wrapped in bacon, then served on squares of toast.

─── INGREDIENTS ───

Serves 4
16 cooked and shelled mussels
juice of 1 lemon
about 30ml/2 tbsp Worcestershire
   sauce
few drops Tabasco sauce
8 slices streaky bacon
lemon wedges and toast or bread,
   to serve

1 Place the mussels in a bowl with the lemon juice, Worcestershire sauce and Tabasco sauce, lightly toss the mussels, then cover and leave in a cool place for 30 minutes.

2 Meanwhile, stretch each slice of bacon with the back of a knife, then cut each slice across in half.

3 Preheat the grill (broiler). Remove the mussels from the bowl, then wrap a piece of bacon around each one. Secure each wrapped mussel with a wooden cocktail stick (toothpick).

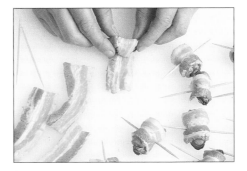

4 Place the wrapped mussels on a grill rack and cook under the grill (broiler) for 3–5 minutes, until the bacon is crisp, turning frequently. Remove the cocktail sticks (toothpicks) before serving with lemon wedges and toast or bread.

GLAMORGAN SAUSAGES

These tasty sausages are ideal for vegetarians as they are made from cheese and leeks rather than meat.

─── INGREDIENTS ───

Makes 8
150g/5oz/2½ cups fresh breadcrumbs
150g/5oz generous cup grated
   Caerphilly cheese
1 small leek, very finely chopped
15ml/1 tbsp chopped fresh parsley
leaves from 1 thyme sprig, chopped
2 eggs
7.5ml/1½ tsp English mustard
   powder
about 45ml/3 tbsp milk
plain (all-purpose) flour, for coating
15ml/1 tbsp oil
15g/½oz/1 tbsp butter, melted
salt and pepper

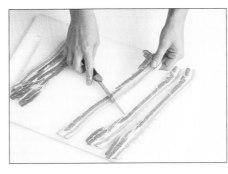

1 Mix the breadcrumbs, cheese, leek, herbs and seasoning. Whisk the eggs with the mustard and reserve 30ml/2 tbsp. Stir the rest into the cheese mixture with enough milk to bind.

2 Divide the cheese mixture into eight and form into sausage shapes.

3 Dip the sausages in the reserved egg to coat. Season the flour, then roll the sausages in it to give a light, even coating. Chill for about 30 minutes until firm.

4 Preheat the grill (broiler) and oil the grill rack. Mix the oil and melted butter together and brush over the sausages. Grill (broil) the sausages for 5–10 minutes, turning carefully occasionally, until golden brown all over. Serve hot or cold.

SAVOURY DISHES

Many dishes that are now popular as supper or lunch dishes, such as Macaroni Cheese and Toad In The Hole, were served at high tea. This meal was eaten at about 6 o'clock and consisted of a savoury dish, usually accompanied by bread and butter, and cake. Other dishes, such as Bacon And Egg Pie and Cornish Pasties, made handy 'edible packages' for farmers and miners respectively, to take into the fields and down the mines for their lunch. Traditional vegetable dishes, often regional and frequently sources of simple, inexpensive meals for the poor, such as Pan Haggerty, also now provide us with the basis of a quick lunch or supper. Many savoury dishes are ideal for vegetarians.

KEDGEREE

Popular for breakfast in Victorian times, Kedgeree has its origins in Khichri, an Indian rice and lentil dish, and is often flavoured with curry powder.

INGREDIENTS

Serves 4

500g/1¼ lb smoked haddock
115g/4oz/generous ½ cup long grain rice
30ml/2 tbsp lemon juice
150ml/5 fl oz/⅔ cup single (light) or soured (sour) cream
pinch of freshly grated nutmeg
pinch of cayenne pepper
2 hard-boiled eggs, peeled and cut into wedges
50g/2oz/4 tbsp butter, diced
30ml/2 tbsp chopped fresh parsley
salt and pepper
parsley sprigs, to garnish

1 Poach the haddock, just covered by water, for about 10 minutes, until the flesh flakes easily. Lift the fish from the cooking liquid using a slotted spoon, then remove any skin and bones flake the flesh.

2 Pour the rice into a measuring jug and note the volume, then tip out, pour the fish cooking liquid into the jug and top up with water, until it measures twice the volume of the rice.

3 Bring the fish cooking liquid to the boil, add the rice, stir, then cover and simmer for about 15 minutes, until the rice is tender and the liquid absorbed. While the rice is cooking, preheat the oven to 180°C/350°F/ Gas 4, and butter a baking dish.

4 Remove the rice from the heat and stir in the lemon juice, cream, flaked fish, nutmeg and cayenne. Add the egg wedges to the rice mixture and stir in gently.

5 Tip the rice mixture into the baking dish, dot with butter and bake for about 25 minutes.

6 Stir the chopped parsley into the Kedgeree, check the seasoning and garnish with parsley sprigs.

COOK'S TIP
Taste the Kedgeree before you add salt, since the smoked haddock may already be quite salty.

BUBBLE AND SQUEAK

The name is derived from the bubbling of the vegetables as they boiled for their first cooking, and the way they squeak when they are fried.

INGREDIENTS

60ml/4 tbsp dripping, bacon fat or oil
1 onion, finely chopped
450g/1 lb potatoes, cooked and
  mashed
225g/8oz cooked cabbage or Brussels
  sprouts, finely chopped
salt and pepper

1 Heat half the dripping, fat or oil in a heavy frying pan. Add the onion and cook, stirring frequently, until softened, but not browned.

2 Mix together the potatoes, cabbage or sprouts and season to taste with salt and plenty of pepper.

3 Add the vegetables to the pan, stir well, then press the vegetable mixture into a large, even cake.

4 Cook over a moderate heat for about 15 minutes, until the cake is browned underneath.

5 Hold a large plate over the pan, then invert the vegetable cake on to it. Add the remaining fat or oil to the pan, then, when hot, slip the cake back into the pan, browned side uppermost.

6 Cook the Bubble and Squeak over a moderate heat for a further 10 minutes or so, until the underside of the cake is golden brown, then serve hot, cut into wedges.

COOK'S TIP
If you don't have left-over, cooked cabbage or brussels sprouts, use fresh raw vegetables instead. Shred the cabbage first and cook both in boiling salted water until just tender. Drain thoroughly, then chop and continue from step 2.

MACARONI CHEESE WITH LEEKS

Leeks add a new twist and extra flavour to an ever-popular family favourite.

INGREDIENTS

Serves 4
175g/6oz/1½ cups short-cut
* macaroni*
50g/2oz/4 tbsp butter
4 leeks, chopped
60ml/5 tbsp plain (all-purpose) flour
750ml/1¼ pints/3 cups milk
200g/7oz/scant 2 cups grated mature
* Cheddar cheese*
45ml/3 tbsp fresh breadcrumbs
salt and pepper

COOK'S TIP
The sauce can be flavoured with mustard or chopped herbs, such as parsley, chives or thyme.

---

1 Preheat the oven to 200°C/400°F/ Gas 6. Cook the macaroni in plenty of boiling salted water for 8–10 minutes, until tender. Drain well.

2 Melt the butter in a saucepan, add the leeks and cook, stirring occasionally, for about 4 minutes. Stir in the flour, cook for 1 minute, then remove the pan from the heat.

3 Gradually stir the milk into the pan, then return to the heat and bring to the boil, stirring. Simmer for about 3 minutes.

4 Remove from the heat and stir in the macaroni and most of the cheese, and season to taste. Pour the macaroni mixture into a baking dish. Mix together the breadcrumbs and the remaining cheese, then sprinkle over the dish. Bake for 20–25 minutes, until the topping is golden.

BROCCOLI AND STILTON PUFF

Cauliflower can be used instead of broccoli in this dish, or if you like, you can use a mixture of the two.

INGREDIENTS

Serves 4
675g/1½ lb broccoli
4 eggs, separated
115g/4oz blue Stilton cheese,
* crumbled*
about 10ml/2 tsp wholegrain or
* French mustard*
salt and pepper

1 Preheat the oven to 190°C/375°F/ Gas 5. Thoroughly butter a 19cm/7½ in soufflé dish.

2 Cook the broccoli in boiling salted water until just tender. Drain the broccoli, refresh under cold running water, then drain well.

3 Place the broccoli in a food processor with the egg yolks and process until smooth. Tip the mixture into a bowl then mix in the Stilton and add mustard and seasoning to taste.

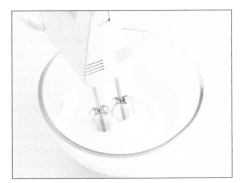

4 Whisk the egg whites until stiff but not dry, then gently fold into the broccoli mixture in three batches. Transfer the broccoli mixture to the dish and bake for about 35 minutes, until risen, just set in the centre, and golden. Serve immediately.

TOAD IN THE HOLE

Sausages are cooked in a light batter which rises to a crisp, brown crust, making this a tasty and substantial supper dish.

INGREDIENTS

Serves 4

90g/3½oz/scant 1 cup plain
 (all-purpose) flour
30ml/2 tbsp chopped fresh parsley
10ml/2 tsp chopped fresh thyme
1 egg, beaten
300ml/½ pint/1¼ cups milk and water,
 mixed
60ml/4 tbsp oil
450g/1 lb good-quality sausages
salt

1 Stir the flour, herbs and salt together in a bowl and form a well in the centre.

2 Pour the egg into the well, then gradually pour in the milk and water while stirring the dry ingredients into the liquids. Beat to form a smooth batter, then leave for 30 minutes.

3 Preheat the oven to 220°C/425°F/ Gas 7. Pour the oil into a small roasting tin (pan) or baking dish, add the sausages, turn them to coat them thoroughly in the oil, then cook the sausages in the oven for 10–15 minutes, until they are beginning to brown all over and the oil is very hot.

4 Stir the batter using a wooden spoon, then remove the roasting tin (pan) or baking dish from the oven and quickly pour the batter over the sausages and return the roasting tin (pan) or baking dish to the oven to bake for about 40 minutes (depending on the depth of the batter), until well risen and crisp around the edges.

COOK'S TIP
It is important to preheat the oil with the sausages so that the batter rises well and becomes crisp.

CORNISH PASTIES

There are many traditional recipes for pasties, which were the original packed lunch, but usually people just used to add whatever was available.

INGREDIENTS

Makes 6
500–675g/1¼–1½lb ready-made
   shortcrust (pie) pastry
450g/1lb chuck steak, diced
1 potato, about 175g/6oz, diced
175g/6oz swede (rutabaga), diced
1 onion, chopped
2.5ml/½ tsp dried mixed herbs
a little beaten egg, to glaze
salt and pepper

1 Preheat the oven to 220°C/425°F/
Gas 7. Divide the pastry into six equal pieces, then roll out each piece to a 20cm/8 in round.

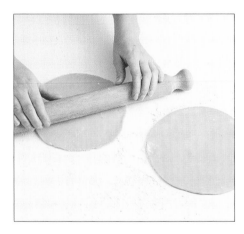

2 Mix together the steak, vegetables, herbs and seasoning, then spoon an equal amount on to one half of each pastry round.

> COOK'S TIP
> Other vegetables, such as turnip, carrot or celery could be used in place of the swede (rutabaga), if you prefer.

3 Brush the pastry edges with water, then fold the free half of each round over the filling. Press the edges firmly together to seal.

4 Use a fish slice to transfer the pasties to a baking (cookie) sheet, then brush each one with beaten egg.

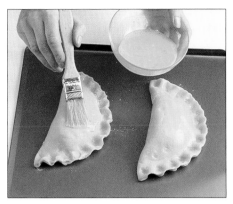

5 Bake the pasties for 15 minutes, then reduce the oven temperature to 160°C/325°F/Gas 3 and bake for a further hour. Serve hot or cold.

SAVOURY POTATO CAKES

Serve hot on their own with a salad, and a dollop of soured (sour) cream, plain yogurt or tomato sauce, if you like.

INGREDIENTS

Serves 4
450g/1 lb potatoes, grated
1 small onion, grated
2 slices streaky bacon, finely chopped
30ml/2 tbsp self-raising (self-rising) flour
2 eggs, beaten
oil, for frying
salt and pepper

1 Rinse the potatoes, drain and pat dry, then mix with the onion, bacon, flour, eggs and seasoning.

2 Heat a 1cm/½ in layer of oil in a frying pan (skillet), then add about 15ml/1 tbsp of the potato mixture and quickly spread the mixture out with the back of the spoon.

3 Add a few more spoonfuls of the mixture in the same way, leaving space between each one, and cook for 4–5 minutes, until golden underneath.

4 Turn the cakes over and cook for 3–4 minutes until the other side is golden brown. Lift the potato cakes out of the pan and transfer to a heated serving dish and keep warm while frying the remaining potato mixture in the same way.

PAN HAGGERTY

Serve this Northumberland dish cut into wedges for a snack, supper or light lunch, accompanied by a crisp salad.

INGREDIENTS

Serves 4
60ml/4 tbsp oil
450g/1 lb firm potatoes, thinly sliced
1 large onion, thinly sliced
115g/4oz/1 cup grated mature Cheddar cheese
salt and pepper

COOK'S TIP
Use any well flavoured hard cheese, in place of the Cheddar.

1 Heat the oil in a large, heavy frying pan. Remove the pan from the heat and arrange alternate layers of potato, onion and cheese, starting and ending with a layer of potatoes, and seasoning each layer.

2 Cook for 30 minutes, starting over a low heat and then increasing it so the underside of the mixture browns. Meanwhile, preheat the grill (broiler).

3 Place the pan under the grill (broiler) for 5–10 minutes to brown the top of the Pan Haggerty. Slide the Pan Haggerty on to a warm plate and cut into wedges.

EGGS WITH SPINACH AND CHEESE SAUCE

If fresh spinach is not available, thaw 450g/1 lb frozen spinach and squeeze it hard to expel surplus liquid; use in the recipe from step 4.

INGREDIENTS

Serves 4

1kg/2 lb fresh spinach, stalks removed
40g/1½oz/3 tbsp butter or margarine
45ml/3 tbsp plain (all-purpose) flour
300ml/½ pint/1¼ cups milk
75g/3oz/¾ cup grated mature Cheddar cheese
pinch of English mustard powder
large pinch of freshly grated nutmeg
4 hard-boiled eggs, peeled and halved lengthways
salt and pepper

1 Wash but do not dry the spinach, then place in a large saucepan with just the water clinging to the leaves. Cook until the spinach is wilted and no free liquid is visible. Tip the spinach into a sieve (strainer) and squeeze out as much liquid as possible, then chop.

2 Melt 25g/1oz/2 tbsp of the butter or margarine in a saucepan, stir in the flour, cook for 1 minute, then remove from the heat. Gradually add the milk, stirring constantly, then return to the heat and bring to the boil, stirring. Simmer gently for about 4 minutes.

3 Remove from the heat and stir in 50g/2oz/4 tbsp cheese, the mustard and seasoning. Preheat the grill (broiler).

4 Melt the remaining butter in a small saucepan, then stir in the spinach, nutmeg and seasoning and warm through. Transfer the spinach to a shallow baking dish and arrange the egg halves on top in a single layer.

5 Pour the sauce over the eggs, sprinkle with the remaining cheese and place under the grill (broiler) until golden and bubbling.

BACON AND EGG PIE

Serves 4
*450–500g/1–1¼lb ready-made
  shortcrust (pie) pastry*
beaten egg or milk, to glaze

For The Filling
30ml/2 tbsp oil
*4 slices smoked bacon, cut into 4cm/
  1½in pieces*
1 small onion, finely chopped
5 eggs
*22.5ml (1½ tbsp) chopped fresh parsley
  (optional)*
salt and pepper

1 Butter a deep 20cm/8in flan tin
(quiche pan). Roll out two-thirds of
the pastry on a lightly floured surface
and use to line the flan tin (quiche
pan). Cover the pastry case and chill
for 30 minutes.

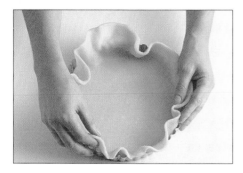

2 Preheat the oven to 200°C/400°F/
Gas 6. In a small heavy pan, cook
the oil and bacon until the bacon fat
begins to run, then add the onion and
cook gently until soft. Transfer to
kitchen paper to drain and cool.

> **COOK'S TIP**
> This pie can be made in a flan
> ring placed on a baking (cookie)
> sheet, if preferred.

3 Cover the bottom of the pastry case
with the bacon mixture, spreading
it evenly, then break the eggs on to the
bacon, spacing them evenly apart.
Carefully tilt the flan tin (quiche pan)
so the egg whites flow together.
Sprinkle the eggs with the chopped
fresh parsley, if used, plenty of black
pepper, and just a little salt if the
bacon is very salty. Place a baking
(cookie) sheet in the oven to heat.

4 Roll out the remaining pastry,
dampen the edges and place over
the pie case. Roll over the top with a
rolling pin, remove excess pastry and
use for pastry leaves. Brush pie with
egg and make a hole in the centre.

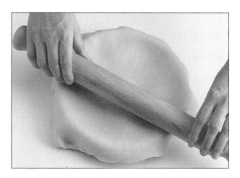

5 Place the pie on the baking (cookie)
sheet and bake for 10 minutes, then
reduce the oven temperature to 180°C/
350°F/Gas 4 and bake for 20 minutes.
Leave to cool before cutting.

Baked Eggs With Asparagus

This recipe makes a little asparagus serve six people. If you cook the eggs so the yolks are still soft, they form a delicious sauce for the asparagus and prawns (shrimp).

— Ingredients —

Serves 6

175g/6oz asparagus
50g/2oz shelled prawns (shrimp),
   chopped
6 eggs
90ml/6 tbsp whipping (light) cream
30ml/3 tbsp finely grated mature
   Cheddar Cheese
salt and pepper

1 Preheat the oven to 180°C/350°F/ Gas 4. Butter six 9cm/3½ in ramekin dishes and place in a shallow baking tin (pan).

2 Trim off woody parts from the asparagus, then steam asparagus for 4 minutes, until half cooked.

3 Reserve six tips, chop the remaining asparagus and divide among the ramekins with the prawns (shrimp), then carefully break an egg into each.

4 Season the eggs, then gently spoon 15ml/1 tbsp of cream on to each and lightly spread it out to cover the top completely. Place an asparagus tip on top of each.

5 Sprinkle the cheese over the asparagus and cream, pour boiling water into the baking tin to come halfway up the sides of the dishes, then bake for 12–15 minutes until the eggs are set to the required degree.

Eggs In Baked Potatoes

— Ingredients —

Serves 4

4 large baking potatoes
40g/1½oz/3 tbsp butter
30ml/2 tbsp hot single (light) cream
   or milk
30ml/2 tbsp snipped fresh chives
4 eggs
about 50g/2oz/½ cup finely grated
   mature Cheddar cheese
salt and pepper

1 Preheat the oven to 200°F/400°C/ Gas 6. Bake the potatoes for about 1½ hours, until soft.

2 Working quickly, cut a slice about a quarter to a third of the way from the top of each potato, then scoop the flesh into a bowl, taking care not to pierce the potato skins.

3 Add the butter, cream or milk, chives and seasoning to the bowl and mash the ingredients together.

4 Divide the potato mixture between the potato skins, and make a dip in each with the back of a spoon.

5 Break an egg into each dip, season, then return to the oven for about 10 minutes until the eggs are just set. Sprinkle the cheese over the eggs, then place under the grill (broiler) until golden. Serve immediately.

CAULIFLOWER CHEESE

INGREDIENTS

Serves 4

1 cauliflower, broken into large florets
40g/1½oz/3 tbsp butter
1 small onion, chopped
2 slices streaky bacon, chopped
45ml/3 tbsp plain (all-purpose) flour
450ml/¾ pint/scant 2 cups milk
115g/4oz/1 cup grated mature
   Cheddar cheese
pinch of English mustard powder
salt and pepper

1 Cook the cauliflower in boiling salted water until almost tender. Drain well and tip into a baking dish.

2 Meanwhile, melt the butter in a saucepan and gently cook the onion and bacon until the onion is soft, then spoon over the cauliflower.

3 Stir the flour into the butter in the pan and cook, stirring, for 1 minute. Remove the pan from the heat and slowly pour the milk into the pan, stirring all the time.

4 Return the saucepan to the heat and bring to the boil, stirring constantly. Simmer for 4–5 minutes, stirring occasionally.

5 Preheat the grill (broiler). Remove the pan from the heat and stir in three-quarters of the cheese. Add the mustard and seasoning to taste.

6 Pour the sauce over the cauliflower, sprinkle the remaining cheese over the top and put under the grill (broiler) until the top is golden and bubbling.

GOLDEN CHEESE PUDDING

INGREDIENTS

Serves 4

600ml/1 pint/2½ cups milk
75g/3oz/1¾ cups fresh breadcrumbs
175g/6 oz/1½ cups grated mature
   Cheddar cheese
7.5ml/1½ tsp prepared mustard
4 eggs, separated
salt and pepper

COOK'S TIP
When whisking egg whites, make sure that both the bowl and beaters are clean and dry.

1 Bring the milk to the boil, then stir in the breadcrumbs.

2 Meanwhile, preheat the oven to 180°C/350°F/Gas 4 and butter a 1.5 litre/2½ pint/6¼ cup baking dish.

3 Whisk the egg whites in a large bowl until stiff but not dry, then carefully fold the egg whites into the breadcrumb mixture using a large spoon or a spatula in three batches.

4 Transfer the mixture to the baking dish and bake for about 30–45 minutes, depending on the depth of the dish, until just lightly set and golden.

MEAT DISHES

There has always been a strong meat-eating tradition in Britain, and at times a family's wealth has been judged by the amount of meat consumed. Britain is famed for her roasts, and well-to-do households would choose large prime-quality joints for Sunday lunch. But there are also dishes developed to deal with cheaper cuts or to 'stretch' meat to make it go further – Lancashire Hotpot and Irish Stew are examples, even Yorkshire Pudding was originally intended to be eaten before the Roast Beef to take the edge off the appetite. There are delicious pastry-covered pies like Steak, Kidney And Mushroom Pie, as well as Shepherd's Pie with its potato topping. Country recipes like Pork With Plums and Somerset Pork With Apples and old favourites like Liver And Onions offer plenty of variety on the mainstay roasts and casseroles.

ROAST BEEF WITH YORKSHIRE PUDDING

For this classic Sunday lunchtime meal, choose a joint of beef on the bone, such as sirloin or rib, or a boned and rolled joint of sirloin, rib or topside (top round).

INGREDIENTS

Serves 6

1.75kg/4lb joint of beef
30–60ml/2–4 tbsp dripping or oil
300ml/½ pint/1¼ cups vegetable or veal stock, wine or water
salt and pepper

For The Yorkshire Puddings

50g/2oz/½ cup plain (all-purpose) flour
1 egg, beaten
150ml/¼ pint/⅔ cup mixed water and milk
dripping or oil, for cooking

1 Weigh the beef and calculate the cooking time, allowing 15 minutes per 450g/1lb plus 15 minutes for rare meat, 20 minutes plus 20 minutes for medium and 25–30 minutes plus 25 minutes for well-done.

2 Preheat the oven to 220°C/425°F/Gas 7. Heat the dripping or oil in a roasting tin (pan) in the oven.

3 Place the meat on a rack, fat-side uppermost, then place the rack in the roasting tin (pan).

4 Baste the beef with the dripping or oil, and cook for the required time, basting occasionally.

5 To make the Yorkshire puddings, stir the flour, salt and pepper together in a bowl and form a well in the centre. Pour the egg into the well, then slowly pour in the milk, stirring in the flour to give a smooth batter. Leave to stand for 30 minutes.

6 A few minutes before the meat is ready, spoon a little dripping or oil in each of 12 patty tins and place in the oven until very hot. Remove the meat from the oven, season, then cover loosely with foil and keep warm.

7 Quickly divide the batter among the patty tins, then bake for 15–20 minutes, until well risen and brown.

8 Spoon off the fat from the roasting tin (pan). Add the stock, wine or water, stirring to dislodge the sediment, and boil for a few minutes. Check the seasoning, then serve with the beef and Yorkshire puddings.

BEEF OLIVES

-------- INGREDIENTS --------

Serves 4

25g/1oz/2 tbsp butter
2 slices bacon, finely chopped
115g/4oz mushrooms, chopped
15ml/1 tbsp chopped fresh parsley
grated rind and juice of 1 lemon
115g/4oz/2 cups fresh breadcrumbs
675g/1½ lb topside (top round) of beef,
*   cut into 8 thin slices*
45ml/3 tbsp plain (all-purpose) flour
45ml/3 tbsp oil
2 onions, sliced
450ml/¾ pint/scant 2 cups brown veal
*   stock*
salt and pepper
chopped fresh parsley, to garnish

1 Preheat the oven to 160C°/325°F/
Gas 3. Heat the butter, add the
bacon and mushrooms and fry for
about 3 minutes, then mix them with
the parsley, lemon rind and juice,
breadcrumbs and seasoning.

2 Spread an equal amount of the
breadcrumb mixture evenly over
the beef slices, leaving a narrow border
clear around the edge.

3 Roll up the slices and tie securely
with fine string, then dip the beef
rolls in the flour to coat lightly.

4 Heat the oil in a heavy shallow
pan, then fry the beef rolls until
lightly browned. Remove the beef rolls
from the pan and keep warm.

5 Add the onions to the pan and fry
until browned. Stir in the remaining
flour and cook until lightly browned.
Pour in the stock, stirring constantly,
then bring to the boil, stirring and simmer for 2–3 minutes.

6 Transfer the beef rolls to a
casserole, pour over the sauce, then
cover the casserole tightly and cook in
the oven for 2 hours. Lift out the
'olives' using a slotted spoon and
remove the string. Then return them to
the sauce and serve hot, garnished with
parsley.

┌─────────────────────────────┐
│ COOK'S TIP   │
│ At the end of the cooking the│
│ onions can be pureed with a │
│ little of the stock, then   │
│ stirred back into the   │
│ casserole to make a smooth   │
│ sauce, if you prefer.   │
└─────────────────────────────┘

BEEF IN GUINNESS

INGREDIENTS

Serves 6

1kg/2lb chuck steak, cut into 4cm/
  1½in cubes
plain (all-purpose) flour, for coating
45ml/3 tbsp oil
1 large onion, sliced
1 carrot, thinly sliced
2 celery sticks, thinly sliced
10ml/2 tsp sugar
5ml/1 tsp English mustard powder
15ml/1 tbsp tomato purée (paste)
2.5 x 7.5 cm/1 x 3 in strip orange rind
bouquet garni
600ml/1 pint/2½ cups Guinness
salt and pepper

1 Toss the beef in flour to coat. Heat 30ml/2 tbsp oil in a large, shallow pan, then cook the beef in batches until lightly browned. Transfer to a bowl.

2 Add the remaining oil to the pan, then cook the onions until well browned, adding the carrot and celery towards the end.

3 Stir in the sugar, mustard, tomato purée (paste), orange rind, Guinness and seasoning, then add the bouquet garni and bring to the boil. Return the meat, and any juices in the bowl, to the pan; add water, if necessary, so the meat is covered. Cover the pan tightly and cook gently for 2–2½ hours, until the meat is very tender.

STEAK, KIDNEY AND MUSHROOM PIE

INGREDIENTS

Serves 4

30ml/2 tbsp oil
1 onion chopped
115g/4oz bacon, chopped
500g/1¼ lb chuck steak, diced
30ml/2 tbsp plain (all-purpose) flour
115g/4oz lambs' kidneys
400ml/14fl oz/1⅔ cups beef stock
large bouquet garni
115g/4oz button mushrooms
225g/8oz ready-made puff pastry
beaten egg, to glaze
salt and pepper

1 Preheat the oven to 160°C/325°F/ Gas 3. Heat the oil in a heavy-based pan, then cook the bacon and onion until lightly browned.

2 Toss the steak in the flour. Stir the meat into the pan in batches and cook, stirring, until browned.

3 Toss the kidneys in flour and add to to the pan with the bouquet garni. Transfer to a casserole dish, then pour in the stock, cover and cook in the oven for 2 hours. Stir in the mushrooms and seasoning and leave to cool.

4 Preheat the oven to 220°C/425°F/ Gas 7. Roll out the pastry to 2cm/ ¾ in larger than the top of a 1.2 litre/2 pint/5 cup pie dish. Cut off a narrow strip from the pastry and fit around the dampened rim of the dish. Brush the pastry strip with water.

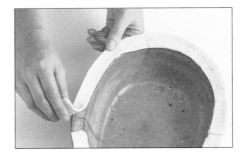

5 Tip the meat mixture, into the dish. Lay the pastry over the dish, press the edges together to seal, then knock them up with the back of a knife.

6 Make a small slit in the pastry, brush with beaten egg and bake for 20 minutes. Lower the oven temperature to 180°C/350°F/Gas 4 and bake for a further 20 minutes, until the pastry is risen, golden and crisp.

SHEPHERD'S PIE

Serves 4

30ml/2 tbsp oil
1 onion, finely chopped
1 carrot, finely chopped
115g/4oz mushrooms, chopped
500g/1¼ lb lean chuck steak, minced
* (ground)*
300ml/½ pint/1¼ cups brown veal
* stock or water*
15ml/1 tbsp plain (all-purpose) flour
bay leaf
10–15ml/2–3 tsp Worcestershire
* sauce*
15ml/1 tbsp tomato purée (paste)
675g/1½ lb potatoes, boiled
25g/1oz/2 tbsp butter
45ml/3 tbsp hot milk
15ml/1 tbsp chopped fresh tarragon
salt and pepper

1 Heat the oil in a saucepan, add the onion, carrot and mushrooms and cook, stirring occasionally, until browned. Stir the beef into the pan and cook, stirring to break up the lumps, until lightly browned.

2 Blend a few spoonfuls of the stock or water with the flour, then stir this mixture into the pan. Stir in the remaining stock or water and bring to a simmer, stirring. Add the bay leaf, Worcestershire sauce and tomato purée (paste), then cover and cook very gently for 1 hour, stirring occasionally. Uncover the pan towards the end of cooking to allow any excess water to evaporate, if necessary.

3 Preheat the oven to 190°C/375°F/ Gas 5. Gently heat the potatoes for a couple of minutes, then mash with the butter, milk and seasoning.

4 Add the tarragon and seasoning to the mince, then pour into a pie dish. Cover the mince with an even layer of potato and mark the top with the prongs of a fork. Bake for about 25 minutes, until golden brown.

IRISH STEW

Serves 4

4 slices smoked streaky bacon,
  chopped
2 celery sticks, chopped
2 large onions, sliced
8 middle neck lamb chops, about
  1kg/2lb total weight
1kg/2lb potatoes, sliced
300ml/½ pint/1¼ cups brown veal
  stock or water
22.5ml/1½ tbsp Worcestershire sauce
5ml/1 tsp anchovy sauce
salt and pepper
chopped fresh parsley, to garnish

1 Preheat the oven to 160°C/325°F/ Gas 3. Fry the bacon for 3–5 minutes until the fat runs, then add the celery and a third of the onions and cook, stirring occasionally, until browned.

2 Layer the lamb chops, potatoes, vegetables and bacon and remaining onions in a heavy flameproof casserole, seasoning each layer, and finishing with a layer of potatoes.

3 Stir the veal stock or water, Worcestershire sauce and anchovy sauce into the bacon and vegetable cooking juices in the pan and bring to the boil. Pour into the casserole, adding water if necessary so the liquid comes half way up the casserole.

4 Cover the casserole tightly, then cook in the oven for 3 hours, until the meat and vegetables are tender. Serve hot, sprinkled with chopped fresh parsley.

COOK'S TIP
The mutton that originally gave the flavour to Irish Stew is often difficult to obtain nowadays, so other flavourings are added to compensate.

SQUAB PIE

INGREDIENTS

Serves 4

675g/1½lb lamb neck fillets, cut into 12
  pieces
115g/4oz gammon, diced
1 onion, thinly sliced
350g/12oz leeks, sliced
1 large cooking apple, peeled, cored
  and sliced
1.25–2.5ml/¼–½tsp ground allspice
1.25–2.5ml/¼–½tsp freshly grated
  nutmeg
150ml/¼ pint/⅔ cup lamb, beef or
  vegetable stock
225g/8oz ready-made shortcrust (pie)
  pastry
beaten egg or milk, to glaze
salt and pepper

1 Preheat the oven to 200°C/400°F/
Gas 6. Layer the meats, onion, leeks
and apple in a 900ml/1½ pint/3¾ cup
pie dish, sprinkling in the spices and
seasoning as you go. Pour in the stock.

2 Roll out the pastry to 2cm/¾ in
larger than the top of the pie dish.
Cut a narrow strip from around the
pastry, fit it around the dampened rim
of the dish, then brush with water.

3 Lay the pastry over the dish, and
press the edges together to seal
them. Brush the top with beaten egg or
milk, and make a hole in the centre.

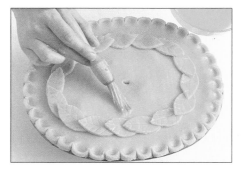

4 Bake the pie for 20 minutes, then
reduce the oven temperature to
180°C/350°F/Gas 4 and continue to
bake for 1-1¼ hours, covering the pie
with foil if the pastry begins to become
too brown.

BEEF WELLINGTON

Beef Wellington is supposedly
so-named because of the resem-
blance of its shape and rich
brown colour to the Duke of
Wellington's boot.

INGREDIENTS

Serves 8

1.4kg/3lb fillet of beef
15g/½oz/1 tbsp butter
30ml/2 tbsp oil
½ small onion, finely chopped
175g/6oz mushrooms, chopped
175g/6oz liver pâté
lemon juice
few drops of Worcestershire sauce
400g/14oz ready-made puff pastry
salt and pepper
beaten egg, to glaze

1 Preheat the oven to 220°C/425°F/
Gas 7. Season the beef with pepper,
then tie it at intervals with string.

2 Heat the butter and oil in a roasting tin
(pan). Brown the beef over a high
heat, then cook in the oven for 20
minutes. Cool and remove the string.

3 Scrape the cooking juices into a
pan, add the onion and mushrooms
and cook until tender. Cool, then mix
with the pâté. Add lemon juice and
Worcestershire sauce.

4 Roll out the pastry to a large
5mm/¼ in thick rectangle. Spread
the pâté mixture on the beef, then
place it in the centre of the pastry.
Damp the edges of the pastry, then fold
over to make a neat parcel, tucking in
the ends neatly; press to seal.

5 Place the parcel on a baking
(cookie) sheet with the join underneath and brush with beaten egg. Bake
for 25–45 minutes, depending how
well done you like the beef to be.

LANCASHIRE HOTPOT

Browning the lamb and kidneys, plus all the extra vegetables and herbs, add flavour to the traditional basic ingredients.

INGREDIENTS

Serves 4

40g/1½oz/3 tbsp dripping, or 45ml/ 3 tbsp oil
8 middle neck lamb chops, about 1kg/2lb total weight
175g/6oz lambs' kidneys, cut into large pieces
1kg/2lb potatoes, thinly sliced
3 carrots, thickly sliced
450g/1lb leeks, sliced
3 celery sticks, sliced
15ml/1 tbsp chopped fresh thyme
30ml/2 tbsp chopped fresh parsley
small sprig of rosemary
600ml/1 pint/2½ cups veal stock
salt and pepper

1 Preheat the oven to 170°C/325°F/ Gas 3. Heat the dripping or oil in a frying pan and brown the chops and kidneys in batches, then reserve the fat.

2 In a large casserole, make alternate layers of lamb chops, kidneys, three-quarters of the potatoes and the carrots, leeks and celery, sprinkling the herbs and seasoning over each layer as you go. Tuck the rosemary sprig down the side.

3 Arrange the remaining potatoes on top. Pour over the stock, brush with the reserved fat, then cover and bake for 2½ hours. Increase the oven temperature to 220°C/425°F/Gas 7. Uncover and cook for 30 minutes.

PORK WITH PLUMS

INGREDIENTS

Serves 4

450g/1lb ripe plums, halved and stoned (pitted)
300ml/½ pint/1¼ cups apple juice
40g/1½oz/3 tbsp butter
15ml/1 tbsp oil
4 pork chops, about 200g/7oz each
1 onion, finely chopped
freshly ground mace
salt and pepper
fresh sage leave, to garnish

1 Heat the butter and oil in a large frying pan and fry the chops until brown on both sides, then transfer them to a plate.

2 Meanwhile, simmer the plums in the apple juice until tender. Strain off and reserve the juice, then purée half the plums with a little of the juice.

3 Add the onion to the pan and cook gently until soft, but not coloured. Return the chops to the pan. Pour over the plum purée and all the juice.

4 Simmer, uncovered, for 10–15 minutes, until the chops are cooked through. Add the remaining plums to the pan, then add the mace and seasoning. Warm the sauce through over a medium heat and serve garnished with fresh sage leaves.

COOK'S TIP
Use boneless pork steaks in place of the chops, if you like.

LIVER AND ONIONS

Calves' liver is wonderfully tender and makes this simple dish mouthwateringly delicious. However it is expensive so substitute thinly sliced lambs' liver, if you prefer and cook over a low heat until just tender.

INGREDIENTS

Serves 4
60ml/4 tbsp oil
3 large onions, total weight about 600g/1lb 6oz, sliced
450g/1lb calves' liver, cut into 5mm/ ¼in thick slices
salt and pepper
sage leaves, to garnish

1 Heat 45 ml/3 tbsp of the oil in a large, heavy frying pan. Add the onions and a little seasoning, cover and cook over a low heat, stirring occasionally, for 25–30 minutes, until the onions are soft.

2 Uncover the pan, increase the heat to medium-high and cook the onions, stirring, for 5–7 minutes until golden. Using a slotted spoon, transfer to a bowl, leaving the oil in the pan.

3 Add the remaining oil to the pan and increase the heat to high. Working in batches so the liver is in a single layer, cook for 45–60 seconds a side until just browned on the outside, and pink inside and tender. Season, then transfer to a warm plate and keep warm while frying the remaining liver in the same way.

4 Return all the liver and the onions to the pan and cook over a high heat for 30–60 seconds. Serve at once, garnished with sage.

COOK'S TIP
The onions need to be covered during their initial cooking, if your frying pan does not have a lid, use foil as a cover.

PORK LOIN WITH CELERY

Serves 4

15ml/1 tbsp oil
50g/2oz/4 tbsp butter
about 1kg/2 lb boned and rolled loin
  of pork, rind removed and well
  trimmed
1 onion, chopped
bouquet garni
3 sprigs fresh dill (dillweed)
150ml/¼ pint/⅔ cup medium-bodied
  dry white wine
150ml/¼ pint/⅔ cup water
sticks from 1 celery head, cut into
  2.5cm/1in lengths
30ml/2 tbsp plain (all-purpose) flour
150ml/¼ pint/⅔ cup double (heavy)
  cream
squeeze of lemon juice
salt and pepper
chopped fresh dill (dillweed), to
  garnish

1 Heat the oil and half the butter in a heavy flameproof casserole just large enough to hold the pork and celery, then add the pork and brown evenly. Transfer the pork to a plate.

2 Add the onion to the casserole and cook until softened but not coloured. Place the bouquet garni and the dill (dillweed) sprigs on the onions, then place the pork on top and add any juices on the plate.

3 Pour the wine and water over the pork, season, cover tightly and simmer gently for 30 minutes.

4 Turn the pork, arrange the celery around it, then re-cover and continue to cook for about 40 minutes, until the pork and celery are tender.

5 Transfer the pork and celery to a warmed serving plate, cover and keep warm. Discard the bouquet garni and dill (dillweed).

6 Mash the remaining butter with the flour, then whisk small pieces at a time into the cooking liquid while it is barely simmering. Cook for 2–3 minutes, stirring occasionally. Stir the cream into the casserole, bring to the boil and add a squeeze of lemon juice.

7 Slice the pork, pour some of the sauce over the slices and garnish with chopped dill (dillweed). Serve the remaining sauce separately.

LAMB WITH MINT SAUCE

INGREDIENTS

Serves 4

8 lamb noisettes, 2–2.5cm/ ¾–1in thick
30ml/2 tbsp oil
45ml/3 tbsp medium-bodied dry white
   wine, or vegetable or veal stock
salt and pepper
sprigs of mint, to garnish

For The Sauce

30ml/2 tbsp boiling water
5–10ml/1–2 tsp sugar
leaves from a small bunch of mint,
   finely chopped
about 30ml/2 tbsp white wine vinegar
salt and pepper

1 For the sauce, stir the water and sugar together, then add the mint, vinegar to taste and seasoning. Leave for 30 minutes.

2 Season the lamb with pepper. Heat the oil in a large frying pan, then fry the lamb, in batches if necessary so the pan is not crowded, for about 3 minutes a side for meat that is pink.

3 Transfer the lamb to a warmed plate and season with salt, then cover and keep warm.

4 Stir the wine or stock into the cooking juices, dislodging the sediment, and bring to the boil. Bubble for a couple of minutes, then pour over the lamb. Garnish the lamb noisettes with small sprigs of mint and serve hot with the Mint Sauce.

SOMERSET PORK WITH APPLES

INGREDIENTS

Serves 4

25g/1oz/2 tbsp butter
500g/1¼lb pork loin, cut into bite-sized
   pieces
12 baby onions, peeled
10ml/2 tsp grated lemon rind
300ml/½ pint/1¼ cups dry (hard) cider
150ml/¼ pint/⅔ cup veal stock
2 crisp eating apples such as Granny
   Smith, cored and sliced
45ml/3 tbsp chopped fresh parsley
100ml/3½ fl oz/scant ½ cup whipping
   cream
salt and pepper

1 Heat the butter in a large sauté or frying pan, then brown the pork in batches. Transfer the pork to a bowl.

2 Add the onions to the pan, brown lightly, then stir in the lemon rind, cider and stock and boil for about 3 minutes. Return all the pork to the pan and cook gently for about 25 minutes, until the pork is tender.

3 Add the apples to the pan and cook for a further 5 minutes. Using a slotted spoon, transfer the pork, onions and apples to a warmed serving dish, cover and keep warm. Stir the parsley and cream into the pan and allow to bubble to thicken the sauce slightly. Season, then pour over the pork and serve hot.

POULTRY AND GAME

At one time almost every household kept at least a few chickens, so it is not surprising that British cooks created an enormous repertoire of chicken dishes. The birds were a source of cheap protein food and provided eggs for the family or for sale. With industrialization, domestic poultry-keeping almost disappeared, and chicken became something of a luxury, but commercial poultry farms now put within everyone's reach not only the classic Stuffed Roast Chicken, but a range of pies such as Chicken Charter Pie and Chicken And Ham Pie, casserole dishes such as Chicken In Green Sauce and Stoved Chicken, as well as Spatchcocked Devilled Poussins and many more. Commercial farming has also made available much game meat and the ingredients for classics like Pot-Roast of Venison are now to be found on the supermarket shelves.

ROAST CHICKEN WITH CELERIAC

INGREDIENTS

Serves 4
1.6kg/3½ lb chicken
15g/½oz/1 tbsp butter

For The Stuffing
450g/1 lb celeriac (celery root),
*   chopped*
25g/1oz/2 tbsp butter
3 slices bacon, chopped
1 onion, finely chopped
leaves from 1 thyme sprig, chopped
leaves from 1 small tarragon sprig,
*   chopped*
30ml/2 tbsp chopped fresh parsley
75g/3oz/1½ cups fresh brown bread-
*   crumbs*
dash of Worcestershire sauce
1 egg
salt and pepper

1 To make the stuffing, cook the cele-riac (celery root) in boiling water until tender. Drain well and chop finely.

2 Heat the butter in a saucepan, then gently cook the bacon and onion until the onion is soft. Stir the celeriac (celery root) and herbs into the pan and cook, stirring occasionally, for 2–3 minutes. Meanwhile, preheat the oven to 200°C/400°F/Gas 6.

COOK'S TIP
Roll any excess stuffing into small balls and bake in an ovenproof dish with the chicken for 20–30 minutes until golden brown.

3 Remove the pan from the heat and stir in the fresh breadcrumbs, Worcestershire sauce, seasoning and sufficient egg to bind. Use to stuff the neck end of the chicken. Season the bird's skin, then rub with the butter.

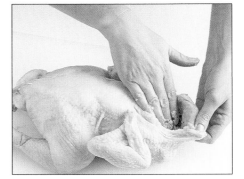

4 Roast the chicken, basting occa-sionally with the juices, for 1¼–1½ hours, until the juices run clear when the thickest part of the leg is pierced.

5 Turn off the oven, prop the door open slightly and allow the chicken to rest for 10 minutes before carving.

STOVED CHICKEN

'Stoved' is derived from the French *étouffer* – to cook in a covered pot – and originates from the Franco/Scottish 'Alliance' of the seventeenth century.

INGREDIENTS

Serves 4

1kg/2 lb potatoes, cut into 5mm/¼ in slices
2 large onions, thinly sliced
15ml/1 tbsp chopped fresh thyme
25g/1oz/2 tbsp butter
15ml/1 tbsp oil
2 large slices bacon, chopped
4 large chicken joints, halved
bay leaf
600ml/1 pint/2½ cups chicken stock
salt and pepper

1 Preheat the oven to 150°C/300°F/ Gas 2. Make a thick layer of half the potato slices in the bottom of a large, heavy casserole, then cover with half the onion. Sprinkle with half the thyme, and seasonings.

COOK'S TIP
Instead of buying large chicken joints and cutting them in half, choose either chicken thighs or chicken drumsticks – or use a mixture of the two.

2 Heat the butter and oil in a large frying pan, then brown the bacon and chicken. Using a slotted spoon, transfer the chicken and bacon to the casserole. Reserve the fat in the pan.

3 Sprinkle the remaining thyme and some seasoning over the chicken, then cover with the remaining onion, followed by a neat layer of overlapping potato slices. Sprinkle with seasoning.

4 Pour the stock into the casserole, brush the potatoes with the reserved fat, then cover tightly and cook in the oven for about 2 hours, until the chicken is tender.

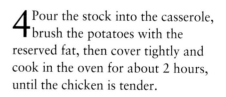

5 Preheat the grill (broiler). Uncover the casserole and place under the grill (broiler) and cook until the slices of potato are beginning to brown and crisp. Serve hot.

CHICKEN WITH LEMON AND HERBS

The herbs can be changed according to what is available; for example, parsley or thyme could be used instead of tarragon and fennel.

INGREDIENTS

Serves 2
50g/2oz/4 tbsp butter
2 spring onions (scallions), white part only, finely chopped
15ml/1 tbsp chopped fresh tarragon
15ml/1 tbsp chopped fresh fennel
juice of 1 lemon
4 chicken thighs
salt and pepper
lemon slices and herb sprigs, to garnish

1 Preheat the grill (broiler) to moderate. In a small saucepan, melt the butter, then add the spring onions (scallions), herbs, lemon juice and seasoning.

2 Brush the chicken thighs generously with the herb mixture, then grill (broil) for 10–12 minutes, basting frequently with the herb mixture.

3 Turn over the chicken and baste again, then cook for a further 10–12 minutes or until the chicken juices run clear.

4 Serve the chicken garnished with lemon slices and herb sprigs, and accompanied by any remaining herb mixture.

CHICKEN WITH RED CABBAGE

INGREDIENTS

Serves 4
50g/2oz/4 tbsp butter
4 large chicken portions, halved
1 onion, chopped
500g/1¼ lb red cabbage, finely shredded
4 juniper berries, crushed
12 cooked chestnuts
120ml/4 fl oz/½ cup full-bodied red wine
salt and pepper

1 Heat the butter in a heavy flame-proof casserole and lightly brown the chicken pieces. Transfer to a plate.

2 Add the onion to the casserole and fry gently until soft and light golden brown. Stir the cabbage and juniper berries into the casserole, season and cook over a moderate heat for 6–7 minutes, stirring once or twice.

3 Stir the chestnuts into the casserole, then tuck the chicken pieces under the cabbage so they are on the bottom of the casserole. Pour in the red wine.

4 Cover and cook gently for about 40 minutes until the chicken juices run clear and the cabbage is very tender. Check the seasoning and serve.

CHICKEN IN GREEN SAUCE

Slow, gentle cooking makes the chicken succulent and tender.

INGREDIENTS

Serves 4
25g/1oz/2 tbsp butter
15ml/1 tbsp olive oil
4 chicken portions
1 small onion, finely chopped
150ml/¼ pint/⅔ cup medium-bodied
    dry white wine
150ml/¼ pint/⅔ cup chicken stock
175g/6oz watercress, leaves removed
leaves from 2 thyme sprigs and 2
    tarragon sprigs
150ml/¼ pint/⅔ cup double (heavy)
    cream
salt and pepper
watercress leaves, to garnish

1 Heat the butter and oil in a heavy shallow pan, then brown the chicken evenly. Transfer the chicken to a plate using a slotted spoon and keep warm in the oven.

2 Add the onion to the cooking juices in the pan and cook until softened but not coloured.

3 Stir in the wine, boil for 2–3 minutes, then add the stock and bring to the boil. Return the chicken to the pan, cover tightly and cook very gently for about 30 minutes, until the chicken juices run clear. Then transfer the chicken to a warm dish, cover the dish and keep warm.

4 Boil the cooking juices hard until reduced to about 60ml/4 tbsp. Remove the leaves from the watercress and herbs, add to the pan with the cream and simmer over a medium heat until slightly thickened.

5 Return the chicken to the casserole, season and heat through for a few minutes. Garnish with watercress leaves to serve.

COOK'S TIP
Use boneless turkey steaks in place of the chicken portions in this recipe, if you prefer.

SPATCHCOCKED DEVILLED POUSSINS

'Spatchcock', perhaps a corruption of the old Irish phrase 'despatch a cock', refers to birds that are split and skewered flat for cooking.

INGREDIENTS

Serves 4

15ml/1 tbsp English mustard powder
15ml/1 tbsp paprika
15ml/1 tbsp ground cumin
20ml/4 tsp tomato ketchup (catsup)
15ml/1 tbsp lemon juice
65g/2½oz/5 tbsp butter, melted
4 poussins, about 450g/1 lb each
salt

1 Mix together the mustard, paprika, cumin, ketchup (catsup), lemon juice and salt until smooth, then gradually stir in the butter.

2 Using game shears or strong kitchen scissors, split each poussin along one side of the backbone, then cut down the other side of the backbone to remove it.

3 Open out a poussin, skin side uppermost, then press down firmly with the heel of your hand. Pass a long skewer through one leg and out through the other to secure the bird open and flat. Repeat with the remaining birds.

4 Spread the mustard mixture evenly over the skin of the birds. Cover loosely and leave in a cool place for at least 2 hours. Preheat a grill (broiler).

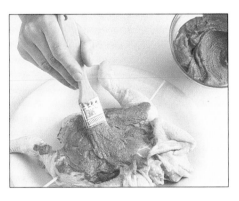

5 Place the birds, skin side uppermost, under the grill (broiler) and cook for about 12 minutes. Turn the birds over, baste with any juices in the pan, and cook for a further 7 minutes, until the juices run clear.

> COOK'S TIP
> Spatchcocked poussins cook very well on the barbecue, make sure the coals are very hot, then cook for 15–20 minutes, turning and basting frequently.

Rabbit With Mustard

Serves 4

15ml/1 tbsp plain (all-purpose) flour
15ml/1 tbsp English mustard powder
4 large rabbit joints
25g/1oz/2 tbsp butter
30ml/2 tbsp oil
1 onion, finely chopped
150ml/¼ pint/⅔ cup beer
300ml/½ pint/1¼ cups chicken or veal
   stock
15ml/1 tbsp tarragon vinegar
30ml/2 tbsp dark brown sugar
10–15ml/2–3 tsp prepared English
   mustard
salt and pepper

To Finish

50g/2oz/4 tbsp butter
30ml/2 tbsp oil
50g/2 oz/1 cup fresh breadcrumbs
15ml/1 tbsp snipped fresh chives
15ml/1 tbsp chopped fresh tarragon

1 Preheat the oven to 160°C/325°F/ Gas 3. Mix the flour and mustard powder together, then put on a plate.

2 Dip the rabbit joints in the flour mixture, reserve excess flour. Heat the butter and oil in a heavy flame-proof casserole, then brown the rabbit. Transfer to a plate. Stir in the onion and cook until soft.

3 Stir any reserved flour mixture into the casserole, cook for 1 minute, then stir in the beer, stock and vinegar. Bring to the boil and add the sugar and pepper. Simmer for 2 minutes.

4 Return the rabbit and any juices that have collected on the plate, to the casserole, cover tightly and cook in the oven for 1 hour.

5 Stir the prepared mustard and salt to taste into the casserole, cover again and cook for a further 15 minutes.

6 To finish, heat together the butter and oil in a frying pan and fry the breadcrumbs, stirring frequently, until golden, then stir in the herbs. Transfer the rabbit to a warmed serving dish, sprinkle over the breadcrumb mixture and serve hot.

Turkey Hotpot

Serves 4

115g/4oz kidney beans, soaked
   overnight and drained
40g/1½oz/3 tbsp butter
2 herby pork sausages
450g/1 lb turkey casserole meat
3 leeks, sliced
2 carrots, finely chopped
4 tomatoes, chopped
10–15ml/2–3 tsp tomato purée (paste)
bouquet garni
400ml/14 fl oz/1⅔ cups chicken stock
salt and pepper

1 Cook the beans in boiling water for 40 minutes, then drain well.

2 Meanwhile, heat the butter in a flameproof casserole, then cook the sausages until browned and the fat runs. Drain on kitchen paper, stir the turkey into the casserole and cook until lightly browned all over, then transfer to a bowl using a slotted spoon. Stir the leeks and carrot into the casserole and brown lightly.

3 Add the tomatoes and tomato purée (paste) and simmer gently for about 5 minutes.

4 Chop the sausages and return to the casserole with the beans, turkey, bouquet garni, stock and sea-soning. Cover and cook gently for about 1¼ hours, until the beans are tender and there is very little liquid.

CHICKEN CHARTER PIE

Since this dish comes from Cornwall, typically cream is used in the filling.

———— INGREDIENTS ————

Serves 4

50g/2oz/4 tbsp butter
4 chicken legs
1 onion, finely chopped
150ml/¼ pint/⅔ cup milk
150ml/¼ pint/⅔ cup soured (sour)
  cream
4 spring onions (scallions), quartered
20g/¾oz fresh parsley leaves, finely
  chopped
225g/8oz ready-made puff pastry
120ml/4 floz/½ cup double (heavy)
  cream
2 eggs, beaten, plus extra for glazing
salt and pepper

1 Melt the butter in a heavy-based, shallow pan, then brown the chicken legs. Transfer to a plate.

2 Add the chopped onion to the pan and cook until softened but not browned. Stir the milk, soured (sour) cream, spring onions (scallions), parsley and seasoning into the pan, bring to the boil, then simmer for a couple of minutes.

3 Return the chicken to the pan with any juices, then cover tightly and cook very gently for about 30 minutes. Transfer the chicken and sauce mixture to a 1.2 litre/2 pint/5 cup pie dish and leave to cool.

4 Meanwhile, roll out the pastry until about 2cm/¾in larger all round than the top of the pie dish. Leave the pastry to relax while the chicken is cooling.

5 Preheat the oven to 220°C/425°F/Gas 7. Cut off a narrow strip around the edge of the pastry, then place the strip on the edge of the pie dish. Moisten the strip, then cover the dish with the pastry. Press the edges together.

6 Make a hole in the centre of the pastry and insert a small funnel of foil. Brush the pastry with beaten egg, then bake for 15–20 minutes.

7 Reduce the oven temperature to 180°C/350°F/Gas 4. Mix the cream and eggs, then pour into the pie through the funnel. Shake the pie to distribute the cream, then return to the oven for 5–10 minutes. Remove the pie from the oven and leave in a warm place for 5–10 minutes before serving, or cool completely if serving cold.

CHICKEN AND HAM PIE

This domed double-crust pie is suitable for a cold buffet, for picnics or any packed meals.

INGREDIENTS

Serves 8
400g/14oz ready-made shortcrust (pie) pastry
800g/1¾ lb chicken breast
350g/12oz uncooked gammon
about 60ml/4 tbsp double (heavy) cream
6 spring onions (scallions), finely chopped
15ml/1 tbsp chopped fresh tarragon
10ml/2 tsp chopped fresh thyme
grated rind and juice of ½ large lemon
5ml/1 tsp freshly ground mace
salt and pepper
beaten egg or milk, to glaze

1 Preheat the oven to 175°C/190°F/ Gas 5. Roll out one-third of the pastry and use it to line a 20cm/8in pie tin (pan) 5cm/2in deep. Place on a baking (cookie) sheet.

2 Mince (grind) 115g/4oz of the chicken with the gammon, then mix with the cream, spring onions (scallions), herbs, lemon rind, 15ml/1tbsp of the lemon juice and the seasoning to make a soft mixture; add more cream if necessary.

3 Cut the remaining chicken into 1cm/½ in pieces and mix with the remaining lemon juice, the mace and seasoning.

4 Make a layer of one-third of the gammon mixture in the pastry base, cover with half the chopped chicken, then add another layer of one-third of the gammon. Add all the remaining chicken followed by the remaining gammon.

5 Dampen the edges of the pastry base. Roll out the remaining pastry to make a lid for the pie.

6 Use the trimmings to make a lattice decoration. Make a small hole in the centre of the pie, brush the top with beaten egg or milk, then bake for about 20 minutes. Reduce the oven temperature to 160°C/325°F/Gas 3 and bake for a further 1-1¼ hours; cover the top with foil if the pastry becomes too brown. Transfer the pie to a wire rack and leave to cool.

CORONATION CHICKEN

INGREDIENTS

Serves 8
½ lemon
2.3kg/5 lb chicken
1 onion, quartered
1 carrot, quartered
large bouquet garni
8 black peppercorns, crushed
salt
watercress sprigs, to garnish

For The Sauce
1 small onion, chopped
15 g/½ oz/1 tbsp butter
15ml/1 tbsp curry paste
15ml/1 tbsp tomato purée (paste)
120ml/4 fl oz/½ cup red wine
bay leaf
juice of ½ lemon, or more to taste
10–15ml/2–3 tsp apricot jam
300ml/½ pint/1¼ cups mayonnaise
120ml/4 fl oz/½ cup whipping cream,
    whipped
salt and pepper

1 Put the lemon half in the chicken cavity, then place the chicken in a saucepan that it just fits. Add the vegetables, bouquet garni, peppercorns and salt.

2 Add sufficient water to come two-thirds of the way up the chicken, bring to the boil, then cover and cook gently for 1½ hours, until the chicken juices run clear.

3 Transfer the chicken to a large bowl, pour over the cooking liquid and leave to cool. When cold, skin and bone the chicken, then chop.

4 Make the sauce, cook the onion in the butter until soft. Add the curry paste, tomato purée (paste), wine, bay leaf and lemon juice, then cook for 10 minutes. Add the jam; sieve and cool.

5 Beat into the mayonnaise. Fold in the cream; add seasoning and lemon juice, then stir in the chicken.

DUCK WITH CUMBERLAND SAUCE

INGREDIENTS

Serves 4
4 duck portions
grated rind and juice of 1 lemon
grated rind and juice of 1 large orange
60ml/4 tbsp redcurrant jelly
60ml/4 tbsp port
pinch of ground mace or ginger
15ml/1 tbsp brandy
salt and pepper
orange slices, to garnish

1 Preheat the oven to 190°C/375°F/ Gas 5. Place a rack in a roasting tin (pan). Prick the duck portions all over, sprinkle with salt and pepper. Place the duck portions on the rack and cook in the oven for 45–50 minutes, until the duck skin is crisp and the juices run clear.

2 Meanwhile, simmer the lemon and orange juices and rinds together in a saucepan for 5 minutes.

3 Stir in the redcurrant jelly until melted, then stir in the port. Bring to the boil, add mace or ginger and seasoning to taste.

4 Transfer the duck to a serving plate; keep warm. Pour the fat from the roasting tin (pan), leaving the cooking juices. With the tin (pan) over a low heat, stir in the brandy, dislodging the sediment and bring to the boil. Stir in the port sauce and serve with the duck, garnished with orange slices.

POT-ROAST OF VENISON

INGREDIENTS

Serves 4–5

1.75kg/4–4½ lb boned joint of
    venison
75ml/5 tbsp oil
4 cloves
8 black peppercorns, lightly crushed
12 juniper berries, lightly crushed
250ml/8 fl oz/1 cup full-bodied red
    wine
115g/4oz lightly smoked streaky
    bacon, chopped
2 onions, finely chopped
2 carrots, chopped
150g/5oz large mushrooms, sliced
15ml/1 tbsp plain (all-purpose) flour
250ml/8 fl oz/1 cup veal stock
30ml/2 tbsp redcurrant jelly
salt and pepper

1 Put the venison in a bowl, add half the oil, the spices and wine, cover and leave in a cool place for 24 hours, turning the meat occasionally.

2 Preheat the oven to 160°C/325°F/ Gas 3. Remove the venison from the bowl and pat dry. Reserve the marinade. Heat the remaining oil in a shallow pan, then brown the venison evenly. Transfer to a plate.

3 Stir the bacon, onions, carrots and mushrooms into the pan and cook for about 5 minutes. Stir in the flour and cook for 2 minutes, then remove from the heat and stir in the marinade, stock, redcurrant jelly and seasoning. Return to the heat, bring to the boil, stirring, then simmer for 2–3 minutes.

4 Transfer the venison and sauce to a casserole, cover and cook in the oven, turning the joint occasionally, for about 3 hours, until tender.

PHEASANT WITH MUSHROOMS

INGREDIENTS

Serves 4

1 pheasant, jointed
250ml/8 fl oz/1 cup red wine
45ml/3 tbsp oil
60ml/4 tbsp Spanish sherry vinegar
1 large onion, chopped
2 slices smoked bacon, cut into strips
350g/12oz chestnut (brown)
    mushrooms, sliced
3 anchovy fillets, soaked for 10
    minutes and drained
350ml/12 fl oz/1½ cups game, veal or
    chicken stock
bouquet garni
salt and pepper

1 Place the pheasant in a dish, add the wine, half the oil and half the vinegar, and scatter over half the onion. Season, then cover and leave in a cool place for 8–12 hours, turning the pheasant occasionally.

2 Preheat the oven to 160°C/325°F/ Gas 3. Lift the pheasant from the dish, pat dry. Reserve the marinade.

3 Heat the remaining oil in a flame-proof casserole, then brown the pheasant joints. Transfer to a plate.

4 Add the bacon and remaining onion to the casserole and cook until the onion is soft. Stir in the mush-rooms and cook for about 3 minutes.

5 Stir in the anchovies and remaining vinegar, boil until reduced. Add the marinade, cook for 2 minutes, then add the stock and bouquet garni. Return the pheasant to the casserole, cover and bake for about 1½ hours. Transfer the pheasant to a serving dish. Boil the cooking juices to reduce. Discard the bouquet garni. Pour over the pheasant and serve at once.

FISH AND SEAFOOD

Britain is surrounded by good sea-fishing waters and has an abundance of rivers, streams and lakes teeming with freshwater fish. Yet the British eat relatively little fish, and traditional recipes feature surprisingly few varieties. Consumption in the past was far greater, but declined after the abolition of compulsory fish days, which once banned meat-eating on sometimes as many as three days a week. British favourites include recipes like Mackerel With Gooseberry Sauce and Herrings In Oatmeal With Mustard Sauce. In other recipes, plainly cooked, succulent fish is accompanied by classic sauces for instance, Haddock With Parsley Sauce and Cod With Caper Sauce. Besides warming casseroles and pies, there are homely dishes like Fish Cakes, and party pieces such as Salmon with Cucumber Sauce.

Haddock With Parsley Sauce

As the fish has to be kept warm while the sauce is made, take care not to overcook it.

INGREDIENTS

Serves 4
4 haddock fillets, about 175g/6oz each
50g/2oz/4 tbsp butter
150ml ¼ pint/⅔ cup milk
150ml/¼ pint/⅔ cup fish stock
1 bay leaf
20ml/4 tsp plain (all-purpose) flour
60ml/4 tbsp cream
1 egg yolk
45ml/3 tbsp chopped fresh parsley
grated rind and juice of ½ lemon
salt and pepper

1 Place the fish in a frying pan, add half the butter, the milk, fish stock, bay leaf and seasoning, and heat over a low-medium heat to simmering point. Lower the heat, cover the pan and poach the fish for 10–15 minutes, depending on the thickness of the fillets, until the fish is tender and the flesh just begins to flake.

2 Transfer the fish to a warmed serving plate, cover the fish and keep warm while you make the sauce. Return the cooking liquid to the heat and bring to the boil, stirring. Simmer for about 4 minutes, then remove and discard the bay leaf.

3 Melt the remaining butter in a saucepan, stir in the flour and cook, stirring, for 1 minute. Remove from the heat and gradually stir in the fish cooking liquid. Return to the heat and bring to the boil, stirring. Simmer for about 4 minutes, stirring frequently. Discard the bay leaf.

4 Remove the pan from the heat, blend the cream into the egg yolk, then stir into the sauce with the parsley. Reheat gently, stirring, for a few minutes; do not allow to boil.

5 Remove from the heat and add the lemon juice and rind, and season to taste. Pour into a warmed sauceboat and serve with the fish.

MACKEREL WITH GOOSEBERRY SAUCE

Gooseberries and mackerel are a classic combination; the tart flavour of the sauce offsets the richness of the fish.

INGREDIENTS

Serves 4

15g/½ oz/1 tbsp butter
225g/8oz gooseberries, topped and
   tailed
4 fresh mackerel, about 350g/12oz
   each, cleaned
1 egg, beaten
pinch of ground mace or ginger, or
   a few drops of orange flower
   water (optional)
salt and pepper
flat leaf parsley, to garnish

1 Melt the butter in a saucepan, add the gooseberries, then cover and cook over a low heat, shaking the pan until the gooseberries are just tender.

2 Meanwhile, preheat the grill (broiler). Season the fish inside and out with salt and black pepper.

3 Cut 2 or 3 slashes in the skin on both sides of each mackerel, then grill (broil) for 15–20 minutes until cooked, turning once.

COOK'S TIP
For the best flavour, look for triple strength orange flower water, which can be obtained from chemists and good food shops.

4 Purée the gooseberries with the egg in a food processor or blender, or mash the gooseberries thoroughly in a bowl with the egg. Press the gooseberry mixture through a sieve (strainer).

5 Return the gooseberry mixture to the pan and reheat gently, stirring, but do not allow to boil. Add the mace, ginger or orange flower water, if using, and seasoning to taste. Serve hot with the mackerel.

HERRINGS IN OATMEAL WITH MUSTARD

INGREDIENTS

Serves 4

about 15ml/1 tbsp Dijon mustard
about 7.5ml/1½ tsp tarragon vinegar
175ml/6 fl oz/¾ cup thick mayonnaise
4 herrings, about 225g/8oz each
1 lemon, halved
115g/4oz/¾ cup medium oatmeal
salt and pepper

1 Beat mustard and vinegar to taste into the mayonnaise. Chill lightly.

2 Place one fish at a time on a board, cut side down and opened out. Press gently along the backbone with your thumbs. Turn over the fish and carefully lift away the backbone.

3 Squeeze lemon juice over both sides of the fish, then season with salt and pepper. Fold the fish in half, skin side outwards.

4 Preheat a grill (broiler) until fairly hot. Place the oatmeal on a plate, then coat each herring evenly in the oatmeal, pressing it in gently.

5 Place the herrings on a grill (broiler) rack and grill (broil) the fish for 3–4 minutes on each side, until the skin is golden brown and crisp and the flesh flakes easily. Serve hot with the mustard sauce, served separately.

FISH AND CHIPS

INGREDIENTS

Serves 4

115g/4oz/1 cup self-raising (self-rising) flour
150ml/¼ pint/⅔ cup water
675g/1½ lb potatoes
675g/1½ lb piece skinned cod fillet, cut into four pieces
oil, for deep frying
salt and pepper
lemon wedges, to serve

1 Stir the flour and salt together in a bowl, then form a well in the centre. Gradually pour in the water, whisking in the flour to make a smooth batter. Leave for 30 minutes.

2 Cut the potatoes into strips about 1cm/½ in wide and 5cm/2 in long, using a sharp knife. Place the potatoes in a colander and rinse them in cold water, then drain and dry well.

3 Heat the oil in a deep-fat fryer or large heavy pan to 150°C/300°F. Using the wire basket, lower the potatoes in batches into the oil and cook for 5–6 minutes, shaking the basket occasionally until the potatoes are soft but not browned. Remove the chips from the oil and drain thoroughly on kitchen paper.

4 Heat the oil in the fryer to 190°C/375°F. Season the fish. Stir the batter, then dip the pieces of fish in turn into it, allowing the excess to drain off.

5 Working in two batches if necessary, lower the fish into the oil and fry for 6–8 minutes, until crisp and brown. Drain the fish on kitchen paper and keep warm.

6 Add the chips in batches to the oil and cook for 2–3 minutes, until brown and crisp. Keep hot. Sprinkle with salt and serve with the fish, accompanied by lemon wedges.

OMELETTE ARNOLD BENNETT

After creating this dish while staying at London's Savoy Hotel, the author, Arnold Bennett, insisted that chefs around the world, wherever he stayed, cooked it for him.

───── INGREDIENTS ─────

Serves 2

175g/6oz smoked haddock fillet, poached and drained
50g/2 oz/4 tbsp butter, diced
175ml/6 fl oz/¾ cup whipping or double (heavy) cream
4 eggs, separated
65g/2½ oz/generous ½ cup grated mature Cheddar cheese
salt and pepper

1 Discard the haddock skin and any bones and flake the flesh.

2 Melt half the butter in 60ml/4 tbsp cream in a fairly small non-stick saucepan, then lightly stir in the fish. Cover, remove from the heat and leave the mixture to cool.

3 Stir together the egg yolks, 15ml/1 tbsp cream and pepper, then lightly stir in the fish mixture. In a separate bowl, mix together the cheese and the remaining cream.

4 Whisk the egg whites until stiff, then fold into the fish mixture.

5 Heat the remaining butter in an omelette pan, add the fish mixture and cook until browned underneath. Pour over the cheese mixture, then grill (broil) until golden and bubbling.

FISH CAKES

For extra-special fish cakes, you could use cooked fresh – or drained, canned – salmon.

───── INGREDIENTS ─────

Serves 4

450g/1 lb cooked, mashed potatoes
450g/1 lb cooked mixed white and smoked fish such as haddock or cod, flaked
25g/1oz/2 tbsp butter, diced
45ml/3 tbsp chopped fresh parsley
1 egg, separated
1 egg, beaten
about 50g/2oz/1 cup fine breadcrumbs made with stale bread
pepper
vegetable oil, for frying

1 Place the potatoes in a bowl and beat in the fish, butter, parsley and egg yolk. Season with pepper.

2 Divide the fish mixture into eight equal portions, then, with floured hands, form each into a flat cake.

3 Beat the remaining egg white with the whole egg. Dip each fish cake in the beaten egg, then in breadcrumbs.

4 Heat the oil in a frying pan, then fry the fish cakes for about 3–5 minutes on each side, until crisp and golden. Drain on kitchen paper and serve hot with a crisp salad.

TROUT WITH HAZELNUTS

The hazelnuts (filberts) in this recipe make an interesting change from the almonds normally used.

INGREDIENTS

Serves 4

50g/2oz/⅓ cup hazelnuts (filberts), chopped
65g/2½oz/5 tbsp butter
4 trout, about 275g/10oz each
30ml/2 tbsp lemon juice
salt and pepper
lemon slices and flat leaf parsley sprigs, to serve

1 Preheat the grill (broiler). Toast the nuts in a single layer, stirring frequently, until the skins split. Then tip the nuts on to a clean tea towel and rub to remove the skins. Leave the nuts to cool, then chop them coarsely.

2 Heat 50g/2oz/4 tbsp of the butter in a large frying pan. Season the trout inside and out, then fry two at a time for 12–15 minutes, turning once, until the trout are brown and the flesh flakes easily when tested with the point of a sharp knife.

MICROWAVE NOTE
You can use a microwave to prepare the nuts, spread them in a shallow dish and cook on full power until the skins split.

3 Drain the cooked trout on kitchen paper, then transfer to a warm serving plate and keep warm while frying the remaining trout in the same way. (If your frying pan is large enough, you could, of course, cook the trout in one batch.)

4 Add the remaining butter to the frying pan, then add the hazelnuts and fry them until evenly browned. Stir the lemon juice into the pan and mix well, then quickly pour the buttery sauce over the trout and serve at once, garnished with slices of lemon and flat leaf parsley sprigs.

TROUT WRAPPED IN A BLANKET

The 'blanket' of streaky bacon bastes the fish during cooking, keeping it moist and adding flavour at the same time.

---INGREDIENTS---

Serves 4
the juice of ½ lemon
4 trout, about 275g/10oz each
4 thyme sprigs
8 thin slices streaky bacon, rinds removed
salt and pepper
chopped fresh parsley and thyme sprigs, to garnish
lemon wedges, to serve

1 Preheat the oven to 200°C/400°F/ Gas 6. Squeeze lemon juice over the skin and in the cavity of each fish, season all over, then put a thyme sprig in each cavity.

2 Stretch each bacon slice using the back of a knife, then wind two slices around each fish.

3 Place the fish in a lightly greased, shallow baking dish with the loose ends of bacon tucked underneath to prevent them unwinding.

4 Bake in the oven for 15–20 minutes, until the trout flesh flakes easily when tested with the point of a sharp knife and the bacon is crisp and beginning to brown.

5 To serve, sprinkle the trout with chopped parsley, then garnish with sprigs of thyme and accompany with lemon wedges.

> **COOK AHEAD**
> The trout can be wrapped in bacon and kept covered in the fridge until ready to cook. Return them to room temperature about 20 minutes before baking.

FISHERMAN'S CASSEROLE

INGREDIENTS

Serves 4–6

450g/1 lb mixed firm fish fillets such
   as cod, haddock and monkfish
50g/2oz/4 tbsp butter
1 onion, sliced
1 celery stick, sliced
350g/12oz potatoes, cut into chunks
750ml/1¼ pints/3⅔ cups fish stock
bouquet garni
150g/5oz frozen broad (fava) beans
300ml/½ pint/1¼ cups milk
115g/4oz peeled prawns (shrimp)
8 shelled (shucked) mussels
salt and pepper
chopped parsley, to garnish

1 Skin the fish and cut the flesh into
bite-sized chunks using a large
sharp knife. Heat the butter in a
saucepan, then fry the onion and celery
until softened but not coloured. Stir
the chunks of potato into the pan and
cook for 1–2 minutes.

2 Add the stock and bouquet garni.
Bring to the boil, cover and simmer
for 20 minutes, until tender.

3 Add the fish, beans and milk and
simmer for 6 minutes, until the fish
flakes. Add the prawns (shrimp),
mussels and seasoning and warm
through. Sprinkle with parsley to serve.

FISH PIE

INGREDIENTS

Serves 4

400ml/14 fl oz/1¾ cups milk
1 bay leaf
¼ onion, sliced
450g/1 lb haddock or cod fillet
225g/8oz smoked haddock fillet
3 hard-boiled eggs, chopped
65g/2½oz/5 tbsp butter
25g/1oz/2 tbsp plain (all-purpose) flour
115g/4oz/1 cup peas
75g/3oz prawns (shrimp) (optional)
30ml/2 tbsp chopped fresh parsley
lemon juice, to taste
500g/1¼ lb potatoes, cooked
60ml/4 tbsp hot milk
60ml/4 tbsp grated Cheddar cheese
salt and pepper

1 Place 350ml/12 fl oz/1½ cups milk,
the bay leaf and onion in a
saucepan, then add the fish. Cover and
poach for 8–10 minutes. Strain and
reserve the milk. Flake the fish into a
pie dish, discarding the skin and any
bones. Add the eggs.

2 Melt 25g/1 oz/2 tbsp butter in a
saucepan, stir in the flour and cook
gently for 1 minute, stirring. Remove
from the heat and stir in the reserved
milk. Return to the heat and bring to
the boil, stirring. Simmer the sauce for
4 minutes, stirring all the time. Remove
from the heat and stir in the peas and
prawns (shrimp).

3 Add the parsley, lemon juice and
seasoning to taste. Pour the sauce
over the fish and eggs and carefully
mix together.

4 Preheat the oven to 180°C/350°F/
Gas 4. Gently heat the remaining
butter in the remaining milk in a small
saucepan, then beat into the potato.
Spoon evenly over the fish and fork up
the surface.

5 Sprinkle the cheese over the pie,
then bake for 25–30 minutes, until
golden. Serve piping hot.

Halibut With Fennel And Orange

Ingredients

Serves 4
1 fennel bulb, thinly sliced
grated rind and juice of 1 orange
150ml/ ¼ pint/ ⅔ cup dry white wine
4 halibut steaks, about 200g/7oz each
50g/2oz/4 tbsp butter
salt and pepper
fennel fronds, to garnish

1 Preheat the oven to 180°C/350°F/ Gas 4. Butter a shallow baking dish.

2 Add the fennel to a saucepan of boiling water, return to the boil and boil for 4–6 minutes, until just tender.

3 Meanwhile, cook the orange rind, juice and wine until reduced by half.

4 Drain the fennel well, then spread in the baking dish and season. Arrange the halibut on the fennel, season, dot with butter, then pour over the reduced orange and wine.

5 Cover and bake for about 20 minutes, until the flesh flakes. Serve garnished with fennel fronds.

Salmon With Cucumber Sauce

Ingredients

Serves 6–8
1.8 kg/4 lb salmon, gutted and scaled
melted butter, for brushing
3 parsley or thyme sprigs
½ lemon, halved
1 large cucumber, peeled
25g/1oz/2 tbsp butter
115ml/4 fl oz/ ½ cup dry white wine
3 tbsp finely chopped fresh dill (dill-
*   weed)*
60ml/4 tbsp soured (sour) cream
salt and pepper

1 Preheat the oven to 220°C/425°F/ Gas 7. Season the salmon and brush inside and out with melted butter. Place the herbs and lemon in the cavity.

2 Wrap the salmon in foil, folding the edges together securely, then bake for 15 minutes. Remove the fish from the oven and leave in the foil for 1 hour, then remove the skin from the salmon.

3 Meanwhile, halve the cucumber lengthways, scoop out the seeds, then dice the flesh.

4 Place the cucumber in a colander, toss lightly with salt, leave for about 30 minutes to drain , then rinse well and pat dry.

5 Heat the butter in a small saucepan, add the cucumber and cook for about 2 minutes, until translucent but not soft. Add the wine to the pan and boil briskly until the cucumber is dry.

6 Stir the dill (dillweed) and soured (sour) cream into the cucumber. Season to taste and serve immediately with the salmon.

COD WITH CAPER SAUCE

The quick and easy sauce with a slightly sharp and 'nutty' flavour is a very effective way of enhancing the fish.

INGREDIENTS

Serves 4

4 cod steaks, about 175g/6oz each
115g/4 oz/½ cup butter
15ml/1 tbsp vinegar from the caper jar
15ml/1 tbsp small capers
15ml/1 tbsp chopped fresh parsley
salt and pepper
tarragon sprigs, to garnish

1 Preheat the grill (broiler). Season the cod. Melt 25g/1oz/2 tbsp of the butter, then brush some over one side of each piece of cod.

2 Grill (broil) the cod for about 6 minutes, turn the fish over, brush with melted butter and cook for a further 5–6 minutes or until the fish flakes easily.

3 Meanwhile, heat the remaining butter until it turns golden brown, then add the vinegar followed by the capers and stir well.

4 Pour the vinegar, butter and capers over the fish, sprinkle with parsley and garnish with the tarragon sprigs.

COOK'S TIP
Thick tail fillets of cod or haddock could be used in place of the cod steaks, if you prefer.

STUFFED PLAICE FILLETS

Serves 4

8 plaice fillets, skinned
115g/4oz/ ½ cup firm cottage cheese,
   drained
few drops Tabasco sauce
grated rind and juice of 1 lemon
90g/3½ oz peeled prawns (shrimp),
   finely chopped
1kg/2 lb spinach, stalks removed
45ml/3 tbsp single (light) cream
25g/1oz/2 tbsp butter, finely diced
pinch of freshly grated nutmeg
30ml/2 tbsp finely grated mature
   Cheddar cheese
salt and pepper

1 Preheat the oven to 180°C/350°F/
Gas 4. Season the fillets of fish and
place skinned-side up on a plate or
chopping board.

2 Mash the cheese with the Tabasco
and the lemon rind and juice. Mix
in the prawns (shrimp).

3 Spread the cheese mixture on the
fillets and roll them up neatly.
Secure with wooden cocktail sticks
(toothpicks).

4 Wash but do not dry the spinach,
place it in a saucepan with just the
water left on the leaves and cook until
no surplus liquid is visible. Tip the
spinach into a sieve (strainer) and press
firmly to expel surplus liquid.

5 Gently heat together the cream,
butter, nutmeg, seasoning and
spinach, then spread in a shallow baking dish just large enough to hold the
fish in a single layer. Put the fish rolls
in the dish and sprinkle them with
cheese. Cover the dish with foil and
bake for 20–25 minutes, until the fish
is tender.

COOK'S TIP
You can use fillets of lemon sole
instead of plaice, if you like.

BRAISED RED CABBAGE

Lightly spiced with a sharp, sweet flavour, braised red cabbage goes well with roast pork, duck and game dishes.

INGREDIENTS

Serves 4–6

1kg/2 lb red cabbage
2 onions, chopped
2 cooking apples, peeled, cored and coarsely grated
5ml/1 tsp freshly grated nutmeg
1.25ml/¼ tsp ground cloves
1.25ml/¼ tsp ground cinnamon
15ml/1 tsp dark brown sugar
45ml/3 tbsp red wine vinegar
25g/1oz/2 tbsp butter or margarine, diced
salt and pepper

1 Preheat the oven to 160°C/325°F/ Gas 3. Cut away and discard the large white ribs from the outer cabbage leaves using a large sharp knife, then finely shred the cabbage.

COOK'S TIP
This recipe can be cooked in advance. Bake the cabbage for 1½ hours, then leave to cool. To complete the cooking, bake in the oven at 160°C/325°F/Gas 3 for about 30 minutes, stirring occasionally.

2 Layer the shredded cabbage in a large ovenproof dish with the onions, apples, spices, sugar and seasoning. Pour over the vinegar and add the diced butter or margarine.

3 Cover the ovenproof dish and cook in the oven for about 1½ hours, stirring a couple of times, until the cabbage is very tender. Serve hot.

LEMONY CARROTS

The carrots are cooked until just tender in lemony stock which is then thickened to make a light, tangy sauce.

---INGREDIENTS---

Serves 4
600ml/1 pint/2½ cups water
450g/1 lb carrots, thinly sliced
bouquet garni
15ml/1 tbsp lemon juice
pinch of freshly grated nutmeg
20g/¾oz/1½ tbsp butter
15ml/1 tbsp plain (all-purpose) flour
salt and pepper

1 Bring the water to the boil in a large pan, then add the carrots, bouquet garni, lemon juice, nutmeg and seasoning and simmer until the carrots are tender.

2 Remove the carrots using a slotted spoon, then keep warm.

3 Boil the cooking liquid hard until reduced to 300ml/½ pint/1¼ cups. Discard the bouquet garni.

4 Mash 15g/½oz/1 tbsp butter and the flour together, then gradually whisk into the simmering reduced cooking liquid, whisking well after each addition, then simmer for about 3 minutes, until the sauce has thickened.

5 Return the carrots to the pan, heat through in the sauce, then remove from the heat, stir in the remaining butter and serve immediately.

BEANS WITH PARSLEY SAUCE

If you grow the herb summer savory, or know someone who does, substitute this for the parsley, as it has a special affinity with broad (fava) beans.

INGREDIENTS

Serves 4
20g/¾oz/1½ tbsp butter
1–1.12 kg/2–2½lb fresh broad (fava) beans, shelled
1 large parsley sprig
150ml/¼pint/⅔ cup double (heavy) or whipping cream
3 egg yolks
few drops of lemon juice
salt and pepper
chopped parsley, to garnish

1 Melt the butter in a saucepan, stir in the beans for 2–3 minutes, then add the parsley, seasoning and enough water barely to cover the beans.

2 Cover the pan tightly, bring just to the boil, then immediately lower the heat and cook very gently, shaking the pan occasionally, for 15–20 minutes until the beans are tender and there is no free liquid. Remove the pan from the heat and leave to cool slightly.

3 Mix the cream with the egg yolks, then stir into the beans. Reheat gently, stirring, until the sauce coats the back of the spoon; do not boil.

4 Add a few drops of lemon juice and garnish with chopped parsley.

BRAISED LETTUCE AND PEAS

Slow, gentle cooking is ideal for older garden peas, but it is also effective with young ones. Serve with lamb or chicken.

INGREDIENTS

Serves 4
25g/1oz/2 tbsp butter
300g/10oz/2 cups shelled fresh peas
8 spring onions (scallions)
1 small firm lettuce, shredded
15ml/1 tbsp chopped fresh parsley
60ml/4 tbsp water
sugar (optional)
salt and pepper

1 Mix the butter, peas, spring onions (scallions), lettuce, parsley, seasoning and water together in a heavy-based saucepan.

2 Cover the pan very tightly and cook very gently for 20–25 minutes, shaking the pan occasionally, until the peas are tender. Should the pan become dry, add just a little water.

3 Taste the peas for seasoning and add a little sugar, if necessary.

Brussels Sprouts with Chestnuts

You really have to wait until late autumn or early winter to enjoy this dish, because fresh chestnuts are one of the few foods that are still seasonal.

Ingredients

350g/12oz fresh chestnuts
300ml/½ pint/1¼ cups chicken or
  vegetable stock (optional)
5ml/1 tsp sugar
675g/1½lb Brussels sprouts
50g/2oz/4 tbsp butter
115g/4oz streaky bacon, cut into strips

1 Cut a cross in the pointed end of each chestnut, then cook in boiling water for 5–10 minutes.

2 Drain the chestnuts, then peel off both the tough outer skin and the finer inner one. Return the chestnuts to the pan, add the stock if using, or water, and sugar and simmer gently for 30–35 minutes, until the chestnuts are tender, then drain thoroughly.

3 Meanwhile, cook the sprouts in boiling salted water for 8–10 minutes, until tender, then drain well.

4 Melt the butter, add the bacon, cook until becoming crisp, then stir in the chestnuts for 2–3 minutes. Add the sprouts and toss together.

Braised Celery

The leaves from the celery can be used as a herb, to flavour soups and casseroles.

Ingredients

Serves 4
40g/1½ oz/3 tbsp butter
2 slices bacon, chopped
1 small onion, finely chopped
1 carrot, finely chopped
1 head of celery, cut into 2.5cm/1in
  lengths
175ml/6 fl oz/¾ cup chicken or
  vegetable stock
bay leaf
parsley sprig
salt and pepper

1 Melt the butter in a large heavy-based saucepan, then cook the bacon, onion and carrot, stirring occasionally, until the vegetables are soft and beginning to colour.

2 Add the celery to the saucepan and cook over a medium heat for 2–3 minutes, stirring occasionally.

3 Stir in the stock, bay leaf, parsley and seasoning and bring to the boil. Cover and simmer gently for about 25 minutes, until the celery is tender and there is almost no liquid left. Serve hot.

> **Cook's Tip**
> If you are cooking this dish for vegetarians, you can omit the bacon and scatter over some chopped toasted almonds instead.

PARSNIPS WITH ALMONDS

Parsnips have an affinity with most nuts, so you could substitute walnuts or hazelnuts (filberts) for the almonds.

INGREDIENTS

Serves 4
450g/1 lb small parsnips
35g/1¼oz/scant 3 tbsp butter
25g/1oz/¼ cup flaked almonds
15ml/1 tbsp soft light brown sugar
pinch of ground mixed spice
15ml/1 tbsp lemon juice
salt and pepper
chopped fresh chervil or parsley, to garnish

1 Cook the parsnips in boiling salted water until almost tender. Drain well. When the parsnips are cool enough to handle, cut each in half across its width. Quarter the wide halves lengthways.

2 Heat the butter in a frying pan. Add the parsnips and almonds and cook gently, stirring and turning the parsnips carefully until they are lightly flecked with brown.

3 Mix together the sugar and mixed spice, sprinkle over the parsnips and stir to mix, then trickle over the lemon juice. Season and heat for 1 minute. Serve sprinkled with chopped fresh chervil or parsley.

COOK'S TIP
You could replace the ground allspice with Chinese five spice powder, if you prefer.

TURNIPS WITH ORANGE

Sprinkle toasted nuts such as flaked almonds or chopped walnuts or hazelnuts (filberts) over the turnips to add a contrasting texture and taste.

INGREDIENTS

Serves 4
50g/2oz/4 tbsp butter
15ml/1 tbsp oil
1 small shallot, finely chopped
450g/1lb small turnips, quartered
300ml/½ pint/1¼ cups freshly squeezed orange juice
salt and pepper

1 Heat the butter and oil in a saucepan, then cook the shallot gently, stirring occasionally, until soft but not coloured.

2 Add the turnips to the shallot and heat, shaking the pan frequently, until the turnips seem to be absorbing the butter and oil.

3 Pour the orange juice on to the turnips, then simmer gently for about 30 minutes, until the turnips are tender and the orange juice reduced to a buttery sauce.

COOK'S TIP
You could add some spice such as ground ginger, cinnamon or crushed cumin seeds.

Spinach and Beetroot Salad

Ingredients

Serves 4–6

45ml/3 tbsp light olive oil
5–6.25ml/1–1¼ tsp caraway seeds
juice of 1 orange
5ml/1 tsp caster (superfine) sugar
675g/1½lb cooked beetroot (beets),
   diced
salt and pepper
young spinach leaves, to serve
chopped fresh parsley, to garnish

1 Arrange the spinach leaves in a shallow salad bowl.

2 Heat the oil in a saucepan, add the caraway seeds, orange juice, sugar and salt and pepper.

3 Add the beetroot (beets) and shake the pan to coat it with the dressing.

4 Spoon the warm beetroot (beets) and dressing mixture in amongst the spinach and sprinkle with the chopped parsley. Serve at once with roast pork, duck or game.

> **Cook's Tip**
> Use freshly cooked beetroot (beets), not those that have been steeped in vinegar.

Beans with Tomatoes

Young runner beans (green beans) should not have 'strings' down the sides, but older ones will and they should be removed before cooking.

Ingredients

Serves 4

675g/1½lb runner (green) beans, sliced
40g/1½oz/3 tbsp butter
4 ripe tomatoes, peeled and chopped
salt and pepper
chopped fresh tarragon, to garnish

> **Cook's Tip**
> French beans can be used instead of runner (green) beans, but reduce the cooking time slightly.

1 Add the beans to a saucepan of boiling water, return to the boil, then boil for 3 minutes. Drain well.

2 Heat the butter in a saucepan and add the tomatoes, beans and seasoning. Cover the pan and simmer gently for 10–15 minutes, until the beans are tender.

3 Tip the beans and tomatoes into a warm serving dish and sprinkle over the chopped tarragon. Serve hot as an accompaniment to grilled meats, poultry or fish.

CHEESE-FILLED BAKED ONIONS

Serve with roast or grilled (broiled) meats, or for a light meal accompanied by a crisp salad and crusty wholemeal or Granary bread.

INGREDIENTS

Serves 4
4 large onions
115g/4oz/1 cup grated mature
   Cheddar cheese
15ml/1 tbsp chopped fresh parsley
40g/1½oz/3 tbsp butter, melted
salt and pepper

1 Peel the onions, then cook in boiling salted water for 15 minutes.

2 Preheat the oven to 180°C/350°F/ Gas 4. Drain the onions, rinse under cold running water, then drain again and cut off the top from each onion using a sharp knife.

> COOK'S TIP
> Substitute another strong flavoured cheese such as blue Stilton, farmhouse Lancashire, or red or blue Cheshire for the mature Cheddar, if you like.

3 Carefully remove the central layers of each onion. Finely chop the scooped-out onion and the onion tops, mix with the cheese, parsley and seasoning, then pile back into the onions.

4 Place the onions in a baking dish, spoon over the butter and bake for about 30 minutes, basting occasionally, until tender.

NEW POTATO AND CHIVE SALAD

The secret of a good potato salad is to mix the potatoes with the dressing while they are still hot so that they absorb it.

INGREDIENTS

Serves 4–6
675g/1½ lb new potatoes (unpeeled)
4 spring onions (scallions)
45ml/3 tbsp olive oil
15ml/1 tbsp white wine vinegar
3.75ml/¾ tsp Dijon mustard
175ml/6 fl oz/¾ cup mayonnaise
45ml/3 tbsp chopped fresh chives
salt and pepper

1 Cook the potatoes in boiling salted water until tender. Meanwhile, finely chop the white parts of the spring onions (scallions) along with a little of the green part.

2 Whisk together the oil, vinegar and mustard. Drain the potatoes well, then immediately toss lightly with the vinegar mixture and spring onions (scallions) and leave to cool.

3 Stir the mayonnaise and chives into the potatoes and chill well until ready to serve with grilled pork, lamb chops or roast chicken.

COOK'S TIP
Look out for the small, waxy potatoes, sold especially for salads and cold dishes – they are particularly good in this recipe.

QUEEN OF PUDDINGS

This pudding was developed from a seventeenth century recipe by Queen Victoria's chefs at Buckingham Palace and named in honour of the monarch.

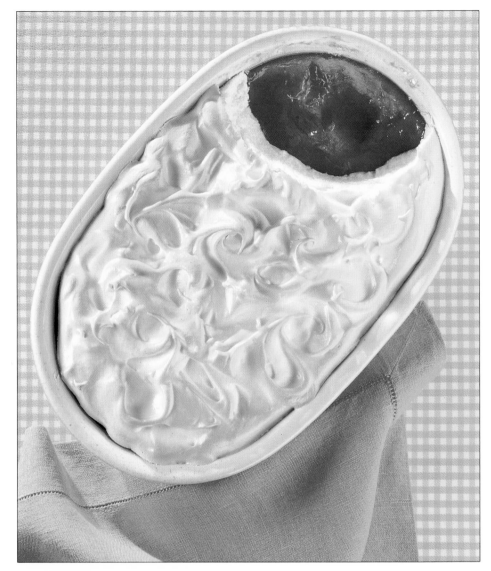

INGREDIENTS

Serves 4
75g/3oz/1½ cups fresh breadcrumbs
60ml/4 tbsp caster (superfine) sugar,
*   plus 5ml/1 tsp*
grated rind of 1 lemon
600ml/1 pint/2½ cups milk
4 eggs
45ml/3 tbsp raspberry jam, warmed

1 Stir the breadcrumbs, 30ml/2 tbsp of the sugar and the lemon rind together in a bowl. Bring the milk to the boil in a saucepan, then stir into the breadcrumbs.

2 Separate three of the eggs and beat the yolks with the whole egg. Stir into the breadcrumb mixture, pour into a buttered baking dish and leave to stand for 30 minutes.

3 Meanwhile, preheat the oven to 160°C/325°F/Gas 3. Bake the pudding for 50–60 minutes, until set.

COOK'S TIP
The traditional recipe calls for raspberry jam, but you may like to ring the changes by replacing it with another flavoured jam, lemon curd, marmalade or fruit purée.

4 Whisk the egg whites in a large, clean bowl until stiff but not dry, then gradually whisk in the remaining 30ml/2 tbsp caster (superfine) sugar until the mixture is thick and glossy, taking care not to overwhip.

5 Spread the jam over the pudding, then spoon over the meringue to cover the top completely. Sprinkle the remaining sugar over the meringue, then bake for a further 15 minutes, until the meringue is beginning to turn a light golden colour.

PEAR AND BLACKBERRY BROWN BETTY

All this delicious fruity pudding needs to go with it is some hot, home-made custard, pouring cream or ice cream.

INGREDIENTS

Serves 4–6
75g/3oz/6 tbsp butter, diced
175g/6oz/3 cups breadcrumbs made
  from 1-day-old bread
450g/1 lb ripe pears
450g/1 lb blackberries
grated rind and juice of 1 small orange
115g/4oz/scant ½ cup demerara sugar
demerara sugar, for sprinkling

1 Preheat the oven to 180°C/350°F/ Gas 4. Heat the butter in a heavy frying pan over a moderate heat, add the breadcrumbs and stir until golden.

2 Peel and core the pears, then cut them into thick slices and mix with the blackberries, orange rind and juice.

3 Mix the demerara sugar with the breadcrumbs, then layer with the fruit in a 900ml/1½ pint/3 cup buttered baking dish, beginning and ending with a layer of sugared breadcrumbs.

4 Sprinkle the extra demerara sugar over the top. Cover the baking dish, then bake the pudding for 20 minutes. Uncover the pudding, then bake for a further 30–35 minutes, until the fruit is cooked and the top brown and crisp.

VARIATION
To make Apple and Raspberry Brown Betty, substitute tart eating apples for the pears and use fresh, but not too ripe, raspberries in place of the blackberries.

BAKED STUFFED APPLES

INGREDIENTS

Serves 4

75g/3oz/scant 1 cup ground almonds
25g/1oz/2 tbsp butter, softened
5ml/1 tsp clear honey
1 egg yolk
50g/2oz/⅓ cup dried apricots, chopped
4 cooking apples, preferably Bramleys

1 Preheat the oven to 200°C/400°F/ Gas 6. Beat together the almonds, butter, honey, egg yolk and apricots.

2 Stamp out the cores from the cooking apples using a large apple corer, then score a line with the point of a sharp knife around the circumference of each apple.

3 Lightly grease a shallow baking dish, then arrange the cooking apples in the dish.

4 Divide the apricot mixture among the cavities in the apples, then bake for 45–60 minutes, until the apples are fluffy.

COOK'S TIP
If cooking apples are unavailable, use four large, tart eating apples.

KENTISH CHERRY BATTER PUDDING

Kent, known as the 'Garden of England', has been particularly well-known for cherries and the dishes made from them.

INGREDIENTS

Serves 4

45ml/3 tbsp kirsch (optional)
450g/1lb dark cherries, pitted
50g/2oz/½ cup plain (all-purpose) flour
50g/2oz/4 tbsp caster (superfine) sugar
2 eggs, separated
300ml/½ pint/1¼ cups milk
75g/3oz/5 tbsp butter, melted
caster (superfine) sugar, for sprinkling

1 Sprinkle the kirsch, if using, over the cherries in a small bowl and leave them to soak for about 30 minutes.

2 Mix the flour and sugar together, then slowly stir in the egg yolks and milk to make a smooth batter. Stir in half the butter and leave for 30 minutes.

3 Preheat the oven to 220°C/425°F/ Gas 7. Pour the remaining butter into a 600 ml/1 pint/2½ cup baking dish and put in the oven to heat.

4 Whisk the egg whites until stiff, then fold into the batter with the cherries and kirsch, if using. Pour into the dish and bake for 15 minutes.

5 Reduce the oven temperature to 180°C/350°F/Gas 4 and bake for 20 minutes, or until golden and set in the centre. Serve sprinkled with sugar.

Sticky Toffee Pudding

INGREDIENTS

Serves 6

*115g/4oz/1 cup toasted walnuts,
   chopped*
175g/6oz/¾ cup butter
175g/6oz/scant 1 cup soft brown sugar
60ml/4 tbsp double (heavy) cream
30ml/2 tbsp lemon juice
2 eggs, beaten
*115g/4oz/1 cup self-raising (self-
   rising) flour*

1 Grease a 900ml/1½ pint/¾ cup
pudding basin and add half the nuts.

2 Heat 50g/2oz/4 tbsp of the butter
with 50g/2oz/4 tbsp of the sugar,
the cream and 15ml/1 tbsp lemon juice
in a small pan, stirring until smooth.
Pour half into the pudding basin, then
swirl to coat it a little way up the sides.

3 Beat the remaining butter and sugar
until light and fluffy, then gradually
beat in the eggs. Fold in the flour and
the remaining nuts and lemon juice and
spoon into the basin.

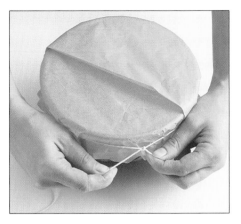

4 Cover the basin with greaseproof
(wax) paper with a pleat folded in
the centre, then tie securely with string.

5 Steam the pudding for about 1¼
hours, until set in the centre.

6 Just before serving, gently warm the
remaining sauce. Unmould the pudding on to a warm plate and pour over
the warm sauce.

Easy Chocolate And Orange Souffles

The base in this soufflé is an
easy-to-make semolina mixture,
rather than the thick white sauce
that most soufflés call for.

INGREDIENTS

Serves 4

50g/2oz/generous ⅓ cup semolina
50g/2oz/scant ¼ cup soft brown sugar
600ml/1 pint/2½ cups milk
grated rind of 1 orange
90ml/6 tbsp fresh orange juice
3 eggs, separated
*65g/2½ oz plain (semi-sweet)
   chocolate, grated*
icing (confectioner's) sugar, for sprinkling

1 Preheat the oven to 200°C/400°F/
Gas 6. Butter a shallow 1.75 litre/
3 pint/7½ cup ovenproof dish.

2 Pour the milk into a heavy-based
saucepan, sprinkle over the semolina
and brown sugar, then heat, stirring
the mixture all the time, until boiling
and thickened.

3 Remove the pan from the heat; beat
in the orange rind and juice, egg
yolks and all but 15ml/1 tbsp of the
grated chocolate.

4 Whisk the egg whites until stiff but
not dry, then lightly fold into the
semolina mixture in three batches.
Spoon the mixture into the dish and
bake for about 30 minutes until just set
in the centre and risen. Sprinkle the top
with the reserved chocolate and the
icing (confectioner's) sugar, then serve
immediately.

PLUM AND WALNUT CRUMBLE

Walnuts add a lovely crunch to the fruit layer in this crumble – almonds would be equally good.

INGREDIENTS

Serves 4–6

75g/3oz/¾ cup walnut pieces
75g/3oz/6 tbsp butter or hard margarine, diced
175g/6oz/1½ cups plain (all-purpose) flour
175g/6oz/scant 1 cup demerara sugar
1kg/2lb plums, halved and stoned (pitted)

1 Preheat the oven to 180°C/350°F/ Gas 4. Spread the nuts on a baking (cookie) sheet and place in the oven for 8–10 minutes, until evenly coloured.

2 Butter a 1.2 litre/2 pint/5 cup baking dish. Put the plums into the dish and stir in the nuts and half of the demerara sugar.

3 Rub the butter or margarine into the flour until the mixture resembles coarse crumbs. Stir in the remaining sugar and continue to rub in until fine crumbs are formed.

4 Cover the fruit with the crumb mixture and press it down lightly. Bake the pudding for about 45 minutes, until the top is golden brown and the fruit tender.

VARIATION
To make Oat and Cinnamon Crumble, substitute rolled oats for half the flour in the crumble mixture and add 2.5–5ml/½–1 tsp ground cinnamon.

BAKED RICE PUDDING

Rice pudding from a can may be convenient, but it does not compare to the tender, creamy home-made version, especially if you like the skin on top.

INGREDIENTS

Serves 4
50g/2oz/¼ cup pudding rice
30ml/2 tbsp soft light brown sugar
50g/2oz/4 tbsp butter
900ml/1½ pints/3¾ cups milk
small strip of lemon rind
freshly grated nutmeg

1 Preheat the oven to 150°C/300°F/ Gas 2. Butter a 1.2 litre/2 pint/5 cup shallow baking dish.

2 Put the rice, sugar and butter into the dish, stir in the milk and lemon rind and sprinkle a little nutmeg over the surface.

3 Bake the rice pudding in the oven for about 2½ hours, stirring after 30 minutes and another couple of times during the next 2 hours until the rice is tender and the pudding has a thick and creamy consistency.

4 If you like skin on top, leave the rice pudding undisturbed for the final 30 minutes cooking (otherwise, stir it again). Serve hot.

VARIATION
Baked rice pudding is even more delicious with fruit, either cooked in it – in which case you might add sultanas (white raisins), raisins or ready-to-eat dried apricots – or, to serve along side, choose sliced fresh peaches or nectarines, raspberries, strawberries or soaked, then lightly poached, prunes.

CABINET PUDDING

INGREDIENTS

Serves 4

25g/1oz/2½ tbsp raisins, chopped
30ml/2 tbsp brandy (optional)
25g/1oz/2½ tbsp glacé (candied)
   cherries, halved
25g/1oz/2 ½ tbsp angelica, chopped
2 trifle sponge cakes, diced
50g/2oz ratafias, crushed
2 eggs
2 egg yolks
30ml/2 tbsp sugar
450ml/¾ pint/1⅞ cups single (light)
   cream or milk
few drops of vanilla essence (extract)

> COOK'S TIP
> The pudding can be cooked in an
> ordinary baking dish, if preferred,
> and served from the dish.

1 Soak the raisins in the brandy, if using, for several hours.

2 Butter a 750ml/1¼ pint/3⅔ cup charlotte mould and arrange some of the cherries and angelica in the base.

3 Mix the remaining cherries and angelica with the sponge cakes, ratafias and raisins and brandy, if using and spoon into the mould.

4 Lightly whisk together the eggs, egg yolks and sugar. Bring the cream or milk just to the boil, then stir into the egg mixture with the vanilla essence

5 Strain the egg mixture into the mould, then leave for 15–30 minutes.

6 Preheat the oven to 160°C/325°F/ Gas 3. Place the mould in a roasting tin (pan), cover with baking paper and pour in boiling water Bake for 1 hour, or until set. Leave for 2–3 minutes, then turn out on to a warm plate.

EVE'S PUDDING

The tempting apples beneath the sponge topping are the reason for the pudding's name.

INGREDIENTS

Serves 4–6

115g/4oz/½ cup butter
115g/4oz/½ cup caster (superfine) sugar
2 eggs, beaten
grated rind and juice of 1 lemon
90g/3½oz/scant 1cup self-raising
   (self-rising) flour
40g/1½ oz/⅓ cup ground almonds
11g/4oz/scant ½ cup soft brown sugar
500–675g 1½ lb cooking apples, cored
   and thinly sliced
25g/1oz/¼ cup flaked almonds

1 Beat together the butter and caster (superfine) sugar in a large mixing bowl until the mixture is very light and fluffy.

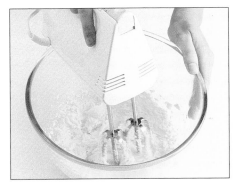

2 Gradually beat the eggs into the butter mixture, beating well after each addition, then fold in the lemon rind, flour and ground almonds.

3 Mix the brown sugar, apples and lemon juice, tip into the dish, add the sponge mixture, then the almonds. Bake for 40–45 minutes, until golden.

BREAD AND BUTTER PUDDING

Vary the dried fruit in this pudding according to your preference. Use currants, sultanas, chopped dried apricots or a mixture of several sorts.

INGREDIENTS

Serves 4–6
75g/3oz/6 tbsp butter
6 slices bread, crusts removed
50g/2oz/about ⅓ cup dried fruit
15ml/1 tbsp chopped mixed (candied) peel
50g/2oz/¼ cup soft light brown sugar
3 eggs, beaten
600ml/1 pint/2½ cups milk

1 Butter a 1.2 litre/2 pint/5 cup baking dish. Butter the bread, then cut off the crusts and cut the slices into triangles, squares or fingers.

2 Arrange half of the bread in the baking dish. Scatter over the dried fruit, mixed peel and half the sugar, then add the remaining bread.

3 Beat the eggs and milk together, then pour into the dish. Sprinkle with the remaining sugar and leave for at least 30 minutes. Meanwhile, preheat the oven to 160°C/325°F/ Gas 3. Bake the pudding for 35–40 minutes until set, and the top is crisp.

COOK'S TIP
For a special occasion, use cream in place of some, or all, of the milk.

APPLE AND ORANGE PIE

INGREDIENTS

Serves 4
400g/14oz ready-made shortcrust (pie) pastry
3 oranges, peeled
1kg/2 lb cooking apples, cored and thickly sliced
30ml/2 tbsp demerara sugar
beaten egg, to glaze
caster (superfine) sugar, for sprinkling

1 Roll out the pastry on a lightly floured surface to 2cm/¾ in larger than the top of a 1.2 litre/2 pint/5 cup pie dish. Cut off a narrow strip around the edge of the pastry and fit on the rim of the pie dish.

COOK'S TIP
Use any excess pastry to make leaves to decorate the pie.

2 Preheat the oven to 190°C/375°F/ Gas 5. Hold one orange at a time over a bowl to catch the juice, cut down between the membranes to remove the segments.

3 Mix the segments and juice, the apples and sugar in the pie dish. Place a pie funnel in the centre of the dish.

4 Dampen the pastry strip. Cover the dish with the rolled out pastry and press the edges to the pastry strip. Brush the top with beaten egg, then bake for 35–40 minutes, until lightly browned. Sprinkle with caster (superfine) sugar before serving.

SURPRISE LEMON PUDDING

The surprise is a delicious, tangy lemon sauce that forms beneath the light topping.

INGREDIENTS

Serves 4

75g/3oz/6 tbsp butter
175g/6oz/⅔ cup soft brown sugar
4 eggs, separated
grated rind and juice of 4 lemons
50g/2oz/½ cup self-raising (self-rising) flour
120ml/4 fl oz/½ cup milk

1 Preheat the oven to 180°C/350°F/ Gas mark 4. Butter an 18cm/7 in soufflé dish or cake tin (pan) and stand it in a roasting tin (pan).

2 Beat the butter and sugar together in a large bowl until pale and very fluffy. Beat in 1 egg yolk at a time, beating well after each addition and gradually beating in the lemon rind and juice until well mixed; do not worry if the mixture curdles a little.

3 Sift the flour and stir into the lemon mixture until well mixed, then gradually stir in the milk.

4 Whisk the egg whites in a separate bowl until stiff but not dry, then lightly, but thoroughly, fold into the lemon mixture in three batches. Carefully pour the mixture into the soufflé dish or cake tin (pan), then pour boiling water around.

5 Bake the pudding in the middle of the oven for about 45 minutes, or until risen, just firm to the touch and golden brown on top. Serve at once.

CASTLE PUDDINGS WITH REAL CUSTARD

─────── INGREDIENTS ───────

Serves 4
about 45ml/3 tbsp blackcurrant,
strawberry or raspberry jam
115g/4oz/½ cup butter
115g/4oz/generous ½ cup caster
(superfine) sugar
2 eggs, beaten
few drops of vanilla essence (extract)
130g/4½oz/generous cup self-raising
(self-rising) flour

For The Custard
450ml/¾ pint/scant 1 cup milk
4 eggs
22.5–30ml/1½–2 tbsp sugar
few drops of vanilla essence (extract)

1 Preheat the oven to 180°C/350°F/ Gas 4. Butter eight dariole moulds. Put about 10ml/2 tsp jam in the base of each mould.

2 Beat the butter and sugar together until light and fluffy, then gradually beat in the eggs, beating well after each addition and adding the vanilla essence (extract) towards the end. Lightly fold in the flour, then divide the mixture among the moulds.

3 Bake the puddings for about 20 minutes until well risen and a light golden colour.

4 Meanwhile, make the sauce. Whisk the eggs and sugar together. Bring the milk to the boil in a heavy, preferably non-stick, saucepan, then slowly pour on to the sweetened egg mixture, stirring constantly.

5 Return the milk to the pan and heat very gently, stirring, until the mixture thickens enough to coat the back of a spoon; do not allow to boil. Cover the pan and remove from the heat.

6 Remove the moulds from the oven, leave to stand for a few minutes, then turn the puddings on to warmed plates and serve with the custard.

COOK'S TIP
Instead of baking the puddings, you can steam them for 30–40 minutes. If you do not have dariole moulds, use ramekin dishes.

GOOSEBERRY AND ELDERFLOWER CREAM

When elderflowers are in season, instead of using the cordial, cook two to three elderflower heads with the gooseberries.

— INGREDIENTS —

Serves 4
500g/1¼ lb gooseberries
300ml/½ pint//1¼ cups double (heavy) cream
about 115g/4 oz/1 cup icing (confectioner's) sugar, to taste
30ml/2 tbsp elderflower cordial or orange flower water (optional)
mint sprigs, to decorate
almond biscuits (cookies), to serve

1 Place the gooseberries in a heavy saucepan, cover and cook over a low heat, shaking the pan occasionally, until the gooseberries are tender. Tip the gooseberries into a bowl, crush them, then leave to cool completely.

2 Beat the cream until soft peaks form, then fold in half the crushed gooseberries. Sweeten and add elderflower cordial, or orange flower water to taste, if used. Sweeten the remaining gooseberries.

3 Layer the cream mixture and the crushed gooseberries in four dessert dishes or tall glasses, then cover and chill. Decorate with mint sprigs and serve with almond biscuits (cookies).

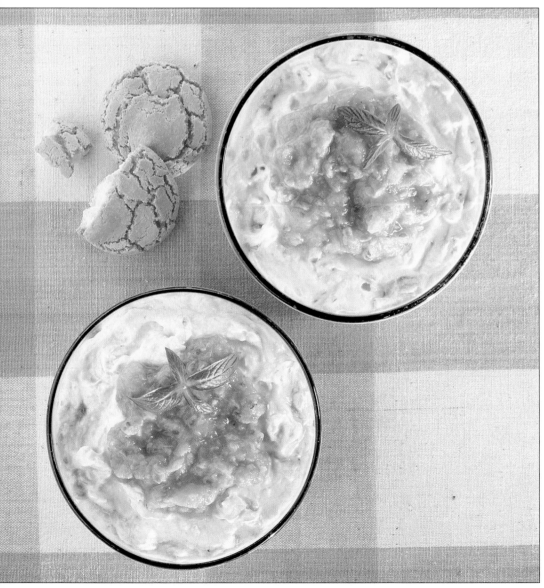

> **COOK'S TIP**
> If preferred, the cooked gooseberries can be puréed and sieved. An equivalent quantity of real custard (see page 132) made with 300ml/½ pint/1¼ cups milk or cream and 2 eggs can replace the cream.

ETON MESS

This dish forms part of the picnic meals parents and pupils enjoy on the lawns at Eton College's annual prize-giving in early June.

INGREDIENTS

Serves 4
500g/1¼ lb strawberries, chopped
45–60ml/3–4 tbsp kirsch
300ml/½ pint/1¼ cups double (heavy) cream
6 small, white meringues,
mint sprigs, to decorate

1 Put the strawberries in a bowl, sprinkle over the kirsch, then cover and chill for 2–3 hours.

2 Whip the cream until soft peaks form, then gently fold in the strawberries with their juices.

3 Crush the meringues into rough chunks, then scatter over the strawberry mixture and fold in gently

4 Spoon the strawberry mixture into a glass serving bowl, decorate with mint sprigs and serve immediately.

COOK'S TIP
If you would prefer to make a less rich version, use strained Greek yogurt or thick natural yogurt instead of part or all of the cream. Simply beat the yogurt gently before adding the strawberries.

CRANACHAN

Serves 4

50g/2oz/⅔ cup medium oatmeal
60ml/4 tbsp clear honey
45ml/3 tbsp whisky
*300ml/½ pint/1¼ cups double (heavy)
    cream*
350g/12oz raspberries
mint sprigs, to decorate

1 Gently warm the honey in the
whisky, then leave to cool.

2 Preheat the grill (broiler). Spread
the oatmeal in a very shallow layer
in the grill (broiler) pan and toast,
stirring occasionally, until browned.
Leave to cool.

3 Whip the cream in a large bowl
until soft peaks form, then gently
stir in the oats, honey and whisky
until well combined.

4 Reserve a few raspberries for decoration, then layer the remainder
with the oat mixture in four tall
glasses. Cover and chill for 2 hours.

5 About 30 minutes before serving,
transfer the glasses to room
temperature. Decorate with the
reserved raspberries and mint sprigs.

OLD ENGLISH TRIFLE

Serves 6

*75g/3oz day-old sponge cake, broken
    into bite-size pieces*
8 ratafias, broken into halves
100ml/3½ fl oz/⅓ cup medium sherry
30ml/2 tbsp brandy
*350g/12oz prepared fruit such as
    raspberries, strawberries or peaches*
*300ml/½ pint/1¼ cups double (heavy)
    cream*
40g/1½oz/⅓ cup toasted flaked almonds
strawberies, to decorate

For The Custard

4 egg yolks
25g/1oz/2 tbsp caster (superfine) sugar
*450ml/¾ pint/scant 2 cups single
    (light) or whipping cream*
few drops of vanilla essence (extract)

1 Put the sponge cake and ratafias in
a glass serving dish, then sprinkle
over the sherry and brandy and leave
until they have been absorbed.

2 To make the custard, whisk the egg
yolks and sugar together. Bring the
cream to the boil in a heavy saucepan,
then pour on to the egg yolk mixture,
stirring constantly.

3 Return the mixture to the pan and
heat very gently, stirring all the
time with a wooden spoon, until the
custard thickens enough to coat the
back of the spoon; do not allow to boil.
Leave to cool, stirring occasionally.

4 Put the fruit in an even layer over
the sponge cake in the serving dish,
then strain the custard over the fruit
and leave to set. Lightly whip the
cream, spread it over the custard, then
chill the trifle well. Decorate with
flaked almonds and strawberries just
before serving.

CHERRY SYLLABUB

This recipe follows the style of
the earliest syllabubs from the
sixteenth and seventeenth
centuries, producing a frothy
creamy layer over a liquid one.

INGREDIENTS

Serves 4
225g/8oz ripe dark cherries, stoned
(pitted) and chopped
30ml/2 tbsp kirsch
2 egg whites
75g/3oz/generous ½ cup caster
(superfine) sugar
30ml/2 tbsp lemon juice
150ml/¼ pint/⅔ cup sweet white wine
300ml/½ pint/1¼ cups double (heavy)
cream

1 Divide the chopped cherries among
six tall dessert glasses and sprinkle
over the kirsch.

2 In a clean bowl, whisk the egg
whites until stiff. Gently fold in the
sugar, lemon juice and wine.

3 In a separate bowl (but using the
same whisk), lightly beat the cream,
then fold into the egg white mixture.

4 Spoon the cream mixture over the
cherries, then chill overnight.

DAMASK CREAM

It is important not to move this
simple, light, yet elegant dessert
while it is setting, otherwise it
will separate.

INGREDIENTS

Serves 4
600ml/1 pint/2½ cups milk
45ml/3 tbsp caster (superfine) sugar
several drops of triple-strength
rosewater
10ml/2 tsp rennet
60ml/4 tbsp double (heavy) cream
sugared rose petals, to decorate
(optional)

1 Gently heat the milk and 30ml/
2 tbsp of the sugar, stirring, until
the sugar has melted and the temperature reaches 36.9°C/98.4°F, or the
milk feels neither hot nor cold.

2 Stir rosewater to taste into the
milk, then remove the pan from the
heat and stir in the rennet.

3 Pour the milk into a serving dish
and leave undisturbed for 2–3
hours, until set.

4 Stir the remaining sugar into the
cream, then carefully spoon over
the junket. Decorate with sugared rose
petals, if liked.

PEACH MELBA

The original dish created for the opera singer Dame Nellie Melba had peaches and ice cream served upon an ice swan.

INGREDIENTS

Serves 4

300g/11oz raspberries
squeeze of lemon juice
icing (confectioner's) sugar, to taste
2 large ripe peaches or 425g/15oz can
  sliced peaches
8 scoops vanilla ice cream

1 Press the raspberries through a non-metallic sieve (strainer).

2 Add a little lemon juice to the raspberry purée and sweeten to taste with icing (confectioner's) sugar.

3 Dip fresh peaches in boiling water for 4–5 seconds, then slip off the skins, halve along the indented line, then slice; or tip canned peaches into a sieve (strainer) and drain.

4 Place two scoops of ice cream in each individual glass dish, top with peach slices, then pour over the raspberry puree. Serve immediately.

COOK'S TIP
If you'd like to prepare this ahead, scoop the ice cream on to a cold baking sheet and freeze until ready to serve, then tansfer the scoops to the dishes.

SUMMER PUDDING

INGREDIENTS

about 8 thin slices day-old white
  bread, crusts removed
800g/1¾lb mixed summer fruits
about 30ml/2 tbsp sugar

1 Cut a round from one slice of bread to fit in the base of a 1.2 litre/ 2 pint/5 cup pudding basin, then cut strips of bread about 5cm/2in wide to line the basin, overlapping the strips slightly so there are no gaps.

2 Gently heat the fruit, sugar and 30ml/2 tbsp water in a large heavy saucepan, shaking the pan occasionally, until the juices begin to run.

3 Reserve about 45ml/3 tbsp fruit juice, then spoon the fruit and remaining juice into the basin, taking care not to dislodge the bread.

4 Cut the remaining bread to fit entirely over the fruit. Stand the basin on a plate and cover with a saucer or small plate that will just fit inside the top of the basin. Place a heavy weight on top. Chill the pudding and the reserved fruit juice overnight.

5 Run a knife carefully around the inside of the basin rim, then invert the pudding on to a cold serving plate. Pour over the reserved juice and serve.

BOODLES ORANGE FOOL

This fool became the speciality of Boodles Club, a gentlemen's club in London's St James's.

INGREDIENTS

Serves 4
4 trifle sponge cakes, cubed
300ml/½ pint/1¼ cups double (heavy) cream
30–60ml/2–4 tbsp caster (superfine) sugar
grated rind and juice of 2 oranges
grated rind and juice of 1 lemon
orange and lemon slices and rind, to decorate

1 Line the bottom and halfway up the sides of a large glass serving bowl or china dish with the cubed trifle sponge cakes.

2 Whip the cream with the sugar until it starts to thicken, then gradually whip in the fruit juices, adding the fruit rinds towards the end.

3 Carefully pour the cream mixture into the bowl or dish, taking care not to dislodge the sponge. Cover and chill for 3–4 hours. Serve decorated with orange and lemon slices and rind.

WATCHPOINT
Take care not to overwhip the cream mixture.

APRICOT AND ORANGE JELLY

INGREDIENTS

Serves 4
350g/12 oz well-flavoured fresh ripe apricots, stoned (pitted)
50–75g/2–3 oz/about ⅓ cup sugar
about 300ml/½ pint/1¼ cups freshly squeezed orange juice
15ml/1 tbsp gelatine
single (light) cream, to serve
finely chopped candied orange peel, to decorate

1 Heat the apricots, sugar and 120ml/4 fl oz/½ cup orange juice, stirring until the sugar has dissolved. Simmer gently until the apricots are tender.

2 Press the apricot mixture through a nylon sieve (strainer) into a small measuring jug.

3 Pour 45 ml/3 tbsp orange juice into a small heatproof bowl, sprinkle over the gelatine and leave for about 5 minutes, until softened.

4 Place the bowl over a saucepan of hot water and heat until the gelatine has dissolved. Slowly pour into the apricot mixture, stirring all the time. Make up to 600ml/1 pint/2½ cups with orange juice.

5 Pour the apricot mixture into four individual dishes and chill until set. Pour a thin layer of cream over the surface of the jellies before serving, decorated with candied orange peel.

Yorkshire Curd Tart

The distinguishing characteristic of Yorkshire curd tarts is all-spice, or 'clove pepper' as it was known locally.

Ingredients

Serves 8

115g/4oz / ½ cup butter, diced
225g/8oz / 2 cups plain (all-purpose) flour
1 egg yolk

For The Filling

large pinch of ground allspice
90g/3½oz / ½ cup soft light brown sugar
3 eggs, beaten
grated rind and juice of 1 lemon
40g/1½oz / 3 tbsp butter, melted
450g/1 lb curd (medium fat soft) cheese
75g/3oz / scant ½ cup raisins or sultanas (white raisins)

1 Toss the butter in the flour, then rub it in until the mixture resembles breadcrumbs. Stir the egg yolk into the flour mixture with a little water to bind the dough together.

2 Turn the dough on to a lightly floured surface, knead lightly and briefly, then form into a ball. Roll out the pastry thinly and use to line a 20cm/8in fluted loose-bottomed flan tin (quiche pan). Chill for 15 minutes.

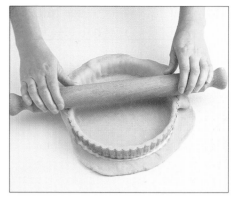

3 Preheat the oven to 190°C/375°F/Gas 5. To make the filling, mix the ground allspice with the sugar, then stir in the eggs, lemon rind and juice, butter, curd cheese and raisins or sultanas (white raisins).

4 Pour the filling into the pastry case, then bake for about 40 minutes until the the pastry is cooked and the filling is lightly set and golden brown. Serve still slightly warm, cut into wedges, with cream, if you like.

COOK'S TIP
Although it's not traditional, you could easily substitute mixed spice for the gound allspice – the flavour will be slightly different, but just as good in this tart.

BAKEWELL TART

Although the pastry base makes this a tart, the original recipe calls it a pudding.

INGREDIENTS

Serves 4

225g/8oz ready-made puff pastry
30ml/2 tbsp raspberry or apricot jam
2 eggs
2 egg yolks
115g/4oz/generous ½ cup caster
  (superfine) sugar
115g/4oz /½ cup butter, melted
50g/2oz /⅔ cup ground almonds
few drops of almond essence (extract)
icing (confectioner's) sugar, for sifting

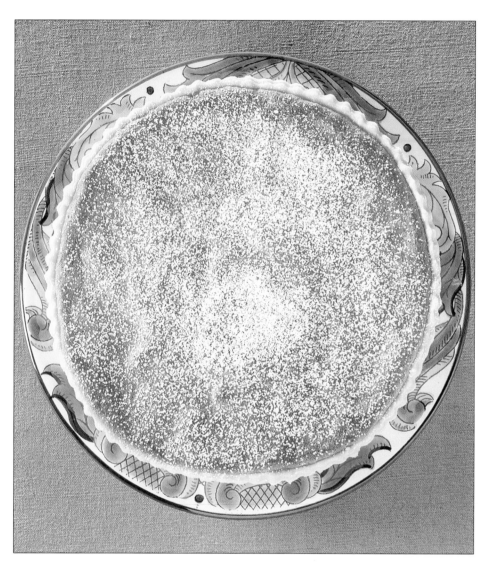

1 Preheat the oven to 200°C/400°F/ Gas 6. Roll out the pastry on a lightly floured surface and use it to line an 18cm/7 in pie plate or loose-based flan tin (quiche pan). Spread the jam over the bottom of the pastry case.

2 Whisk the eggs, egg yolks and sugar together in a large bowl until thick and pale.

3 Gently stir the butter, ground almonds and almond essence (extract) into the mixture.

4 Pour the mixture into the pastry case and bake for 30 minutes, until the filling is just set and browned. Sift icing (confectioner's) sugar over the top before eating hot, warm or cold.

COOK'S TIP
Since this pastry case isn't baked blind first, place a baking sheet in the oven while it preheats, then place the flan tin (quiche pan) on the hot sheet. This will ensure that the bottom of the pastry case cooks right through.

CHOCOLATE CAKE

Ground lightly toasted hazelnuts and finely grated orange rind add an extra-special dimension to this luxurious moist cake.

— INGREDIENTS —

Makes about 10 slices
150g/5oz plain (semi-sweet)
  chocolate, chopped
115g/4oz/½ cup unsalted (sweet)
  butter, chopped
115g/4oz/½ cup caster (superfine)
  sugar
4 eggs, separated
115g/4oz ground lightly toasted
  hazelnuts (filberts)
50g/2oz/1 cup fresh breadcrumbs
grated rind of 1½ oranges
30ml/2 tbsp sieved (strained)
  marmalade, warmed
60ml/4 tbsp chopped hazelnuts
  (filberts), to decorate

For The Icing (Frosting)
150g/5oz plain (semi-sweet)
  chocolate, chopped
50g/2oz/4 tbsp butter, chopped

1 Preheat the oven to 180°C/350°F/ Gas 4. Butter a 23cm/9 in round cake tin (pan) and line the base with greaseproof (wax) paper.

2 Put the chocolate into a small bowl placed over a saucepan of hot water, leave until beginning to melt, then stir until smooth. Remove the bowl from the heat.

3 Beat the butter and sugar together until light and fluffy, then gradually beat in the egg yolks, beating well after each addition; do not worry if the mixture curdles slightly. Beat in the chocolate, then fold in the hazelnuts (filberts), breadcrumbs and orange rind. Whisk the egg whites until stiff but not dry, then fold into the chocolate mixture. Transfer to the cake tin (pan) and bake for 40–45 minutes, until just set in the centre.

4 Remove from the oven, cover with a damp tea towel for 5 minutes, then transfer to a wire rack until cold.

5 To make the icing (frosting), place the chocolate and butter in a bowl over a pan of hot water and stir until smooth. Leave until cool and thick. Spread the cake with marmalade, then spread over the icing (frosting). Scatter over the nuts, then leave to set.

NUTTY CARROT CAKE

Grated carrots are a very traditional addition to cakes and puddings – they add both moisture and colour and produce a moist cake that keeps well.

— INGREDIENTS —

Makes 8–10 slices
225g/8oz/1 cup butter
225g/8oz/generous 1 cup soft light
  brown sugar
4 eggs, separated
grated rind of 1 small orange
15ml/1 tbsp lemon juice
175g/6oz/1½ cups self-raising
  (self-rising) flour
5ml/1 tsp baking powder
50g/2oz/⅔ cup ground almonds
350g/12oz grated carrots
115g/4oz/1 cup walnut pieces

1 Preheat the oven to 180°C/350°F/ Gas 4. Grease and line a 20cm/8in round cake tin (pan) with greaseproof (wax) paper. Beat together the butter and sugar until light and fluffy, then beat in the egg yolks one at a time, beating well after each addition.

2 Stir the orange rind and lemon juice into the butter mixture, followed by the flour, baking powder, ground almonds, carrots and walnuts.

3 Whisk the egg whites until stiff but not dry, then lightly fold into the carrot mixture. Transfer to the tin (pan), make a slight hollow in the centre, then bake for about 1½ hours, until risen and golden; cover the top if it becomes too brown.

4 Leave the cake in the tin (pan) to cool slightly, then turn out on to a wire rack. Remove the lining paper and leave to cool completely.

VARIATION
To make Courgette (Zucchini) And Raisin Cake substitute grated courgettes (zucchini) for the carrots and use raisins in place of the walnut pieces.

MADEIRA CAKE

In the nineteenth century, this cake was served mid-morning with a glass of Madeira wine.

INGREDIENTS

Makes 8–10 slices
175g/6oz/¾ cup butter
175g/6oz/scant 1 cup caster (superfine) sugar
4 eggs, beaten
grated rind of 1 lemon
225g/8oz/2 cups self-raising (self-rising) flour
pinch of salt
2 strips of candied peel

1 Preheat the oven to 180°C/350°F/ Gas 4. Grease and line an 18cm/7in round cake tin (pan).

2 Beat together the butter and sugar until light and fluffy, then gradually beat in the eggs, adding the lemon rind and a little of the flour towards the end. Fold in the remaining flour and the salt, then turn into the prepared cake tin (pan) and smooth the surface.

3 Bake the cake for 30 minutes, until set, then carefully place the peel on the top. Bake for a further 10 minutes, then reduce the oven temperature to 160°C/325°F/Gas 3 and continue to bake until firm in the centre.

4 Leave the cake to cool slightly in the tin (pan), then turn on to a wire rack and carefully remove the lining paper.

MARMALADE TEABREAD

INGREDIENTS

Makes 8–10 slices
200g/7oz/1¾ cups plain (all-purpose) flour
5ml/1 tsp baking powder
6.25ml/1¼ tsp ground cinnamon
90g/3½oz/7 tbsp butter or margarine
50g/2oz/3 tbsp soft light brown sugar
60ml/4 tbsp chunky orange marmalade
1 egg, beaten
about 45ml/3 tbsp milk
60ml/4 tbsp glacé icing and shreds of orange and lemon rind, to decorate

1 Preheat the oven to 160°C/325°F/ Gas 3. Butter a 900ml/1½ pint/3¾ cup loaf tin (pan), then line the base with greased greaseproof (wax) paper.

2 Sift the flour, baking powder and cinnamon together, toss in the butter, then rub in with your fingertips until the mixture resembles breadcrumbs. Stir in the sugar.

3 Mix together the marmalade, egg and most of the milk, then stir into the bowl to make a soft dropping consistency, adding more milk if necessary.

4 Transfer the mixture to the tin (pan) and bake for about 1¼ hours, until firm to the touch. Leave the cake to cool for 5 minutes, then turn on to a wire rack.

5 Carefully peel off the lining paper and leave the cake to cool completely. Drizzle the glacé icing over the top of the cake and decorate with the orange and lemon rinds.

Parkin

The flavour of the cake will improve if it is stored in an airtight container for several days or a week before serving.

Ingredients

Makes 16–20 squares
300ml/ ½ pint/1¼ cups milk
225g/8oz/ ¾ cup golden (corn) syrup
225g/8oz/ ¾ cup black treacle (molasses)
115g/4oz/ ½ cup butter or margarine, diced
50g/2oz/scant ¼ cup dark brown sugar
450g/1 lb/4 cups plain (all-purpose) flour
2.5ml/ ½ tsp bicarbonate of soda (baking soda)
6.25ml/1¼ tsp ground ginger
350g/12oz/4 cups medium oatmeal
1 egg, beaten
icing (confectioner's) sugar, to dust

1 Preheat the oven to 180°C/350°F/ Gas 4. Grease and line the base of a 20cm/8in square cake tin (pan). Gently heat together the milk, syrup, treacle (molasses), butter or margarine and sugar, stirring until smooth; do not boil.

2 Stir together the flour, bicarbonate of soda (baking soda), ginger and oatmeal. Make a well in the centre, pour in the egg, then slowly pour in the warmed mixture, stirring to make a smooth batter.

3 Pour the batter into the tin (pan) and bake for about 45 minutes, until firm to the touch. Cool slightly in the tin (pan), then cool completely on a wire rack. Cut into squares and dust with icing (confectioner's) sugar.

Dorset Apple Cake

Serve this fruity cake warm, and spread with butter if liked.

Ingredients

Makes 6–8 slices
225g/8oz cooking apples, peeled, cored and chopped
juice of ½ lemon
225g/8oz/2 cups plain (all-purpose) flour
7.5ml/1½ tsp baking powder
115g/4oz/ ½ cup butter, diced
165g/5½ oz/scant 1 cup soft light brown sugar
1 egg, beaten
about 30–45 ml/2–3 tbsp milk, to mix
2.5ml/ ½ tsp ground cinnamon

1 Preheat the oven to 180°C/350°F/ Gas 4. Grease and line an 18cm/ 7 in round cake tin (pan).

2 Toss the apple with the lemon juice and set aside. Sift the flour and baking power, rub in the butter, until the mixture resembles breadcrumbs.

3 Stir in 115g/4oz/ ¾ cup of the sugar, the apple and the egg, and mix well, adding sufficient milk to make a soft dropping consistency.

4 Transfer the dough to the prepared tin (pan). In a bowl mix together the remaining sugar and the cinnamon. Sprinkle over the cake mixture, then bake for 45–50 minutes, until golden. Leave to cool in the tin (pan) for 10 minutes, then transfer to a wire rack.

SHORTBREAD

Traditionally the shortbread dough is pressed into decorative wooden moulds, then turned out for baking.

──INGREDIENTS──

Makes 6–8 wedges
115g/4oz/½ cup unsalted (sweet) butter
50g/2oz/4 tbsp caster (superfine) sugar
115g/4oz/1 cup plain (all-purpose) flour
50g/2oz/4 tbsp rice flour

1 Preheat the oven to 160°C/325°F/Gas 3. Place a 15cm/6in plain flan ring on a baking (cookie) sheet.

2 Beat the butter and sugar together until light and fluffy. Stir in the plain (all-purpose) flour and the rice flour, then knead lightly until smooth.

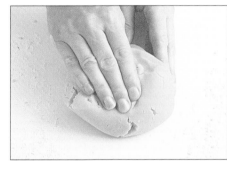

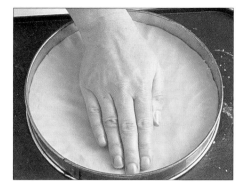

3 Press the dough evenly into the flan ring, then lift the flan ring away. Crimp around the edges of the dough using your thumb and first finger. Prick the surface of the round with a fork, then mark into 6 or 8 wedges.

4 Bake the shortbread dough for 40 minutes, until pale biscuit coloured and just firm to the touch.

5 Leave the shortbread to cool for a few minutes, then carefully transfer to a wire rack to cool completely. To serve, break the shortbread into wedges along the marked lines.

> **COOK'S TIP**
> If you haven't a flan ring, then just roll out the dough until a little larger than a 15cm/6in round, then place a 15cm/6in plate on top and trim the edge neatly with a sharp knife. Remove the plate, crimp the edge of the shortbread and transfer to the baking sheet.

SIMNEL CAKE

This Easter-tide cake keeps well and is best made about six weeks ahead. The balls are said to represent Jesus' faithful apostles.

INGREDIENTS

Makes 8–10 slices

175g/6oz/¾ cup butter
175g/6oz/scant 1 cup soft brown sugar
3 large eggs
225g/8oz/2 cups plain (all-purpose) flour
2.5ml/½ tsp ground cinnamon
2.5ml/½ tsp freshly grated nutmeg
150g/5oz/1 cup currants
150g/5oz/¾ cup sultanas (white raisins)
150g/5oz/¾ cup raisins
75g/3oz/generous ½ cup glacé (candied) cherries, washed, dried and quartered
75g/3oz/generous ½ cup mixed (candied) peel, chopped
grated rind of 1 large lemon
450g/1 lb almond paste
caster (superfine) sugar, for dusting
1 egg white, lightly beaten

1 Preheat the oven to 160°C/325°F/ Gas 3. Grease and line an 18cm/7 in round cake tin (pan). Tie a double layer of brown paper round the outside.

2 Beat the butter and sugar together until pale and fluffy, then gradually beat in the eggs, beating well after each addition. Lightly fold the flour, spices, dried fruits, cherries, mixed (candied) peel and lemon rind into the egg mixture then spoon half the mixture into the tin (pan).

3 Roll half the almond paste to a 16cm/6½ in round on a surface dusted with caster (superfine) sugar. Place the round in the cake tin (pan).

4 Spoon the remaining cake mixture into the tin and bake for 1 hour. Reduce the oven temperature to 150°C/ 300°F/Gas 2 and bake for 2 hours. Leave to cool for 1 hour in the cake tin (pan), then cool on a wire rack.

5 Brush the cake top with egg white. Roll out half the remaining almond paste to a 19cm/7½ in round, place on the cake and crimp. Roll the remaining paste into 11 balls and fix with egg white. Brush the paste with more egg white and grill (broil) until browned.

TANGY LEMON CAKE

INGREDIENTS

Makes about 10 slices
175g/6oz/¾ cup butter
175g/6oz/scant 1 cup caster
(superfine) sugar
3 eggs, beaten
175g/6oz/1½ cups self-raising (self-rising) flour
grated rind of 1 orange
grated rind of 1 lemon

For The Syrup
juice of 2 lemons
115g/4oz/generous ½ cup caster (superfine) sugar

1 Preheat the oven to 180°C/350°F/ Gas 4. Grease a 900g/2 lb loaf tin (pan).

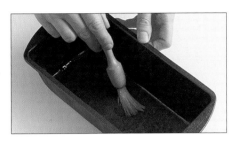

2 Beat the butter and sugar together until light and fluffy, then gradually beat in the eggs. Fold in the flour and the orange and lemon rinds.

3 Turn the cake mixture into the cake tin (pan) and bake for 1¼-1½ hours, until set in the centre, risen and golden.

4 Remove the cake from the oven, but leave it in the tin (pan).

5 To make the syrup, gently heat the sugar in the lemon juice until melted, then boil for 15 seconds. Pour the syrup over the cake and leave to cool.

CHELSEA BUNS

INGREDIENTS

Makes 12
225g/8oz/2 cups strong white flour
½ tsp salt
40g/1½oz/3 tbsp unsalted (sweet) butter
7.5ml/1½ tsp easy-blend yeast
120ml/4 fl oz/½ cup milk
1 egg, beaten
75g/3oz/½ cup mixed dried fruit
25g/1oz/2½ tbsp chopped mixed (candied) peel
50g/2oz/3 tbsp soft light brown sugar
clear honey, to glaze

1 Sift the flour and salt into a bowl, then rub in 25g/1oz/2 tbsp of the butter until the mixture resembles breadcrumbs.

2 Stir in the yeast and make a well in the centre. Slowly pour the milk and egg into the well, stirring the ingredients together, then beat until the dough leaves the sides of the bowl clean.

3 Knead the dough until smooth and elastic. Place in an oiled bowl, cover and leave at room temperature until doubled in volume. Transfer the dough to a floured surface, then roll to a rectangle about 30 x 23cm/12 x 9in.

4 Mix the dried fruits, peel and sugar. Melt the remaining butter and brush over the dough. Scatter over the fruit mixture, leaving a 2.5cm/1in border. Starting at a long side, roll up the dough. Seal the edges, then cut into 12 slices.

5 Place the slices, cut side up, in a greased 18cm/7in square tin (pan). Cover and leave at room temperature until doubled in size.

6 Preheat the oven to 190°C/375°F/ Gas 5. Bake for 30 minutes, until a rich golden brown. Brush the tops with honey and leave to cool slightly in the tin (pan) before turning out.

DROP SCONES

Makes 8–10

115g/4oz/1 cup plain (all-purpose)
*   flour*
5ml/1 tsp bicarbonate of soda (baking
*   soda)*
5ml/1 tsp cream of tartar
25g/1oz/2 tbsp butter, diced
1 egg, beaten
about 150ml/¼ pint/⅔ cup milk

1 Lightly grease a griddle or heavy-based frying pan, then preheat it.

2 Sift the flour, bicarbonate of soda (baking soda) and cream of tartar together, then rub in the butter until the mixture resembles breadcrumbs. Make a well in the centre, then stir in the egg and sufficient milk to give a thick cream consistency.

3 Drop spoonfuls of the mixture, spaced slightly apart, on to the griddle or frying pan. Cook over a steady heat for 2–3 minutes, until bubbles rise to the surface and burst.

4 Turn the scones over and cook for a further 2–3 minutes, until golden underneath. Place the cooked scones in between the folds of a tea towel while cooking the remaining batter. Serve warm, with butter and honey.

COOK'S TIP
Placing the cooked scones in a folded tea towel keeps them soft and moist.

SCONES

Makes 10–12

225g/8oz/2 cups plain (all-purpose) flour
15ml/1 tbsp baking powder
50g/2oz/4tbsp butter, diced
1 egg, beaten
75ml/5 tbsp milk
beaten egg, to glaze

1 Preheat the oven to 220°C/425°F/ Gas 7. Butter a baking (cookie) sheet. Sift the flour and baking powder together, then rub in the butter.

2 Make a well in the centre of the flour mixture, add the egg and milk and mix to a soft dough using a round-bladed knife.

3 Turn out the scone dough on to a floured surface, knead very lightly until smooth.

4 Roll out the dough to about a 2cm/ ¾in thickness and cut into 10 or 12 rounds using a 5cm/2in plain or fluted cutter dipped in flour.

5 Transfer to the baking (cookie) sheet, brush with egg, then bake for about 8 minutes, until risen and golden. Cool slightly on a wire rack then serve with butter, jam and cream.

MELTING MOMENTS

These biscuits (cookies) are very crisp and light – and they melt in your mouth.

─── INGREDIENTS ───

Makes 16–20

40g/1½oz/3 tbsp butter or margarine
65g/2½oz/5 tbsp lard (shortening)
75g/3oz/6 tbsp caster (superfine) sugar
½ egg, beaten
few drops of vanilla or almond essence (extract)
150g/5oz/1¼ cups self-raising (self-rising) flour
rolled oats, for coating
4–5 glacé (candied) cherries, quartered

1 Preheat the oven to 180°C/350°F/ Gas 4. Beat together the butter or margarine, lard (shortening) and sugar, then gradually beat in the egg and vanilla or almond essence (extract).

2 Stir the flour into the beaten mixture, then roll into 16–20 small balls in your hands.

3 Spread the rolled oats on a sheet of greaseproof (wax) paper and toss the balls in them to coat evenly.

4 Place the balls, spaced slightly apart, on 2 baking (cookie) sheets, place a piece of cherry on top of each and bake for 15–20 minutes, until lightly browned.

5 Allow the biscuits (cookies) to cool for a few minutes before transferring to a wire rack to cool completely.

EASTER BISCUITS (COOKIES)

─── INGREDIENTS ───

Makes 16–18

115g/4oz/½ cup butter or margarine
75g/3oz/6 tbsp caster (superfine) sugar, plus extra for sprinkling
1 egg, separated
200g/7oz/1¾ cups plain (all-purpose) flour
2.5ml/½ tsp ground mixed spice
2.5ml/½ tsp ground cinnamon
50g/2oz/scant ½ cup currants
15ml/1 tbsp chopped mixed (candied) peel
15–30ml/1–2 tbsp milk

1 Preheat the oven to 200°C/400°F/ Gas 6. Lightly grease two baking (cookie) sheets.

2 Beat together the butter or margarine and sugar until light and fluffy, then beat in the egg yolk.

3 Sift the flour and spices over the egg mixture, then fold in with the currants and peel, adding sufficient milk to mix to a fairly soft dough.

4 Turn the dough on to a floured surface, knead lightly until just smooth, then roll out using a floured rolling pin, to about 5mm/¼ in thick. Cut the dough into rounds using a 5cm/2in fluted biscuit (cookie) cutter. Transfer the rounds to the baking sheets and bake for 10 minutes.

5 Beat the egg white, then brush over the biscuits (cookies). Sprinkle with caster (superfine) sugar and return to the oven for a further 10 minutes, until golden. Transfer to a wire rack to cool.

INDEX